COLOSSAL
GRAB A PENCIL®
Pocket
FILL-INS

Visit www.pennydellpuzzles.com for more great puzzles

First Bristol Park Books edition published in 2017

Bristol Park Books
252 W. 38th Street
NYC, NY 10018

Bristol Park Books is a registered trademark of Bristol Park
Books, Inc.

Published by arrangement with Penny Publications LLC

ISBN: 978-088486-644-2

Printed in the United States of America

COLOSSAL
GRAB A PENCIL®
Pocket
FILL-INS

RICHARD MANCHESTER

BRISTOL
PARK
BOOKS

HOW TO SOLVE

Fill-In puzzles are crosswords with a delightful difference—we give you all the answers! You solve the puzzle by filling in the diagram with answer words reading across and down as in a crossword puzzle.

The answer words are listed alphabetically according to their lengths. Across and Down words are mixed together. Cross off each word as you use it. When you fill in words in one direction, words in the other direction will automatically be filled in, so remember to cross them off as well.

Each puzzle diagram has one word filled in to help you get started.

PUZZLES

1

3 Letters

ADE
AGE
ALE
EEL
LAG
LEE
NAT
NED
NIL
ODE
OLE
ORR
POI
REN
SHE
VIA

4 Letters

ALDA
ALSO
ANDY
ANTE
ARGO
AUNT
DAHL
DIDI
EDAM
EDNA
ELSA
FOAM
HUNT
HYDE
IDOL
INCA
IRAN
ISLE
JEDI
JOAN
LIAR
LOON
MEAN
NAIL
NAPA
ODIN
OPIE
OSLO
POEM
RANT
SIRE
SOLO
TERI
THAI

5 Letters

ALONE
ATARI
BATHE
CHIRP
CORAL
DARIN
EGRET
ENTER
FIELD
GUISE
HELEN
LLOYD
MANOR

NIECE	VINYL	LAPTOP
OOMPH		MENTAL
PRIDE	**6 Letters**	NOSHER
SLING	ALANIS	
SPARE ✓	CAMERA	**8 Letters**
TIDAL	CELLAR	LANGUAGE
TONER	ENGAGE	OBEDIENT
UNDID	HURRAH	

2

3 Letters

AHA
ELL
ERR
HAL
RAM
SID
USE
WIT

4 Letters

ALEE
ALOE
ALTO
ANKA
ASEA
ASIA
AVOW
AWRY
CAKE
CALS
CARR
DEED
DION
DOLE
DOTE
DRAW
EASE
EVAN
EVEL
GILA
GOAT
GORE
IDLE
IVAN
KALE
KING
LANE
LENA
LENS
LIZA
LOGO
NANA
NEED
ODIE
OVER
OXEN
REEL
SLAB
TEND
UNDO
WHEN
WOVE
YELL
ZONE

5 Letters

AARON
ABLER
ANSON
ARENA
ATLAS
AWARD
BORIC
DIANA
ENSUE
HOARD
INDEX ✓

NASAL	**6 Letters**	ELEVATE
OILER	ANYWAY	GIDDYAP
OSSIE	ENAMEL	MASSAGE
RIVAL	ENERGY	
ROUST	IMPOSE	**8 Letters**
RYDER		NOBLEMAN
TRIKE	**7 Letters**	ONLOOKER
	DAYTIME	

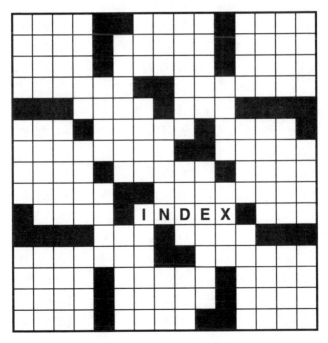

3

3 Letters

AIR
AVA
CAN
EGG
ERE
INA
LOT
NAN
OLD
OWN
REV
RON
TEE
TEN

4 Letters

ALMA
ASHE
ASTA
CLAN
CROC
DIAL
DINO
ELAM
ELLA
EMMY
ERIE
ERLE
FATS
FRAT
HARD
HURL
IFFY
ILSA
KEEL
LARA
LAWN
MEOW
OILY
OINK
OMAR
ONLY
PELE
RELY
RITE
SEAL
SLOB
SLUR
STAR
TEEM
TESH
TORI
UTAH
VEER ✓
WAND
YOLK

5 Letters

AGATE
ANGER
ARRAY
EBERT
EGYPT
ERICA
HOVER
LAHTI
LOGIC
LYNDA

MEDAL	ASTRAY	**7 Letters**
MERYL	CHERUB	MACHETE
REACH	ELAPSE	NOTABLE
STATE	GRATER	UNKNOWN
TULIP	OREGON	
	VIENNA	**8 Letters**
6 Letters	YARROW	ANNOUNCE
ACCORD		TURNOVER

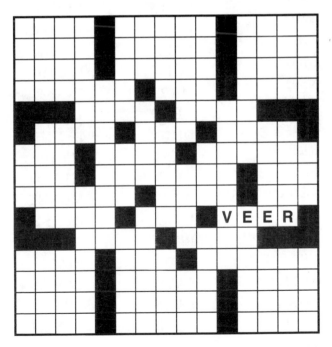

4

3 Letters

ABE
DAM
DAN
DEE
EMO
ENA
GNU
NOD
ORE
PET
RAT

4 Letters

ALAS
ANTI
ARAB
ARTE
AURA
BOSS
CARE
DING
EDEN
ELLY
EMMA
FEAT
GLAD
GRAM
GROW
ILIE
LIRA
LOLA
MART
NERO
OHIO
OKAY
OREL
RAYE
RILE
ROLL
SADA
SALT
SANE
TARP
TART
TATE
TOFU
TOOL

5 Letters

AHEAD
DROVE
EDGAR
EPSOM
GENIE
GRIME
INANE
IRANI
LENIN
MEARA
METRO
MONET
ORDER
RAITT
RIATA
TAMPA ✓
TIMER
TOTEM

WASTE

6 Letters
DENTAL
FEEBLE
SNIVEL
STRAIT

7 Letters
ARSENAL
BILLION
CARFARE
TODDLER

8 Letters
EVACUATE

PERSPIRE
RETAINER
VICINITY

9 Letters
GUIDEBOOK
ORANGUTAN

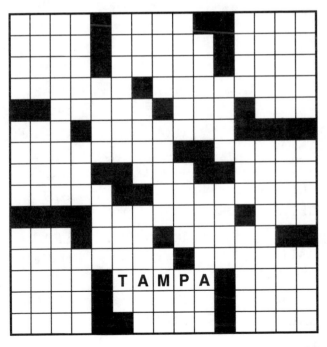

5

3 Letters

BEN
ERA
GOB
RAE
ROE
SIS
TIN
WOK

4 Letters

ANEW
ANNA
ARIA
BETA
BLUR
DALI
DEBT ✓
DEER
EARL

EBAY
ELLE
ELSE
EVEN
EYRE
GWEN
HAVE
HERE
INGA
KNEE
LEST
LORE
MALL
OBOE
ORAL
PAUL
PENN
PLIE
PSST
RAUL
REAL
ROMP
RUST
SOUR

SPUR
STEM
URAL
URGE
WAKE

5 Letters

AERIE
ATTIC
BRETT
BRUCE
CANON
CLASP
CONGO
COUNT
DETER
GRITS
HINGE
LANCE
LEARN
OATER
RAISE
STEAK
TEENY

TRAIT	PATRON	LIBERTY
WEARY	SENTRY	
YOUTH	SHINER	**8 Letters**
	SOOTHE	CROSSBOW
6 Letters	WADERS	PEEKABOO
CAREEN		PROTRUDE
CREWEL	**7 Letters**	TELEGRAM
KENNEL	CYCLONE	

6

3 Digits

103
174
212
244
428
644
654
842
942
985

4 Digits

0206
0309
0429
0484
0733
0804
0936

0955
1291
1447
2085
2272
2564
3029
3031
3289
3297
3681
3895
4132
4494
4575
4728
4747 ✓
5410
5740
5813
5993
6041
6576
7003

7284
8675
8833
8977
9227
9421
9621
9759
9917

5 Digits

00962
25554
35572
37500
40673
41284
41351
41841
42450
43659
47726
72342
72877

77784	487913	9445365
86478	625155	
87968	647014	**8 Digits**
90589	742375	47379587
93473	930043	47420945
		71353921
6 Digits	**7 Digits**	77597922
437016	6233387	

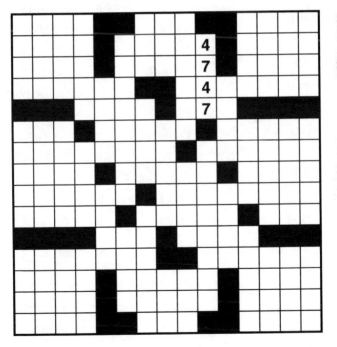

7

3 Letters
ACE
AGE
ARE
ASH
AWE
AWL
BIN
ESS
HAT
MET
PEP
POP
TAP
TWO
UNO
VIE

4 Letters
ABLE

AHEM
ALDA
ALEC
ATOP
AUTO
BUOY
CHUM
CODE
COOK
DOER
EARP
ECRU
FOAM
GEER
GOOD
HOAR
ICON
IDLE
INFO
LOBO
LOCO
LONE
LOPE
MOPE

NOON
NOVA
OVAL
RAVE
SCAD
SEEP
TYPE

5 Letters
ALLOY
ANNOY
BATON
CADET
GEESE
IGLOO
IRISH ✓
NEEDY
OUGHT
OWNER
RIGHT
SCOLD
SCRAM
STOOP
TAUPE

THERE	NAMATH	REGATTA
THESE	RIPPLE	
TRASH	SLIGHT	**8 Letters**
	STAPLE	HEADLINE
6 Letters	STEVIE	IGNORANT
ACCRUE		OKLAHOMA
HERBAL		STILETTO
LOVELY	**7 Letters**	
	ENTITLE	

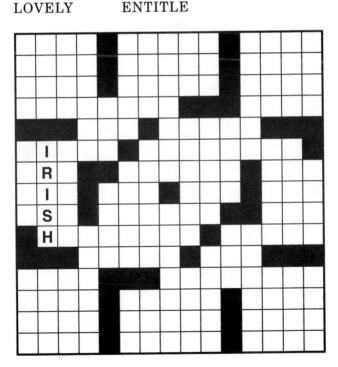

19

8

3 Letters
ADD
APE
END
HUE
ILL
KEN
LON
NEE
RAN
REA
UMA
WOO

4 Letters
AHAB
AIRS
ALMA
ANTE
BAER
CENT
CHAT
COLD
DUCK ✓
DYAN
ECHO
EDIE
ETNA
FOND
GAME
HEAP
IDEA
ISLE
LENA
LENO
LENT
LIME
LION
MATE
MEOW
MILO
NEON
NEST
NINA
OBEY
OBIE
ODOR
OPAL
PASS
POSE
RAKE
REDO
SELA

5 Letters
ARLEN
BRIEF
DRILL
EDDIE
ELDER
HEART
KORAN
MELEE
OSSIE
OTHER
REIGN
SALSA
SLACK

THINK   RANDOM   REEDIER
UNDER   RUCKUS   SCRAPER
          SCHEME   TREADLE
6 Letters TRENCH
BRENDA   **10 Letters**
CHOSEN   **7 Letters** INGREDIENT
ENGINE   CONNORS   NOISEMAKER
MAIDEN   MAHATMA

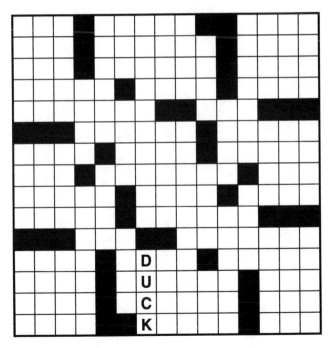

9

3 Letters

ALL
AND
ANT
APT
EAT
EON
GAD
ION
ITT
MAA
ONE
PAY
POI
SAP
TAD
TEE

4 Letters

ALEE
ALOE
ALTO
AMID
AREA
ARGO
ASEA
BEAN
CARR
CHEF
COLA
COST
EDEN
EDGY
ETON
HALT
IDOL
ILIE
ITCH
KETT
LACK
LAMB
MELT
OPIE
OREL
REND
RILE
RITA
ROSA
SWAB
TALE
TERI
TONE
TREE
WAIT
YEAR

5 Letters

ADLAI
ALOHA
ARROW
COMIC ✓
DISCO
EDICT
ENACT
ERASE
GLEAN
NADER
OUNCE

PANEL
PENNY
RADIO
ROOST
ROUGE
SEARS
SENOR
TENOR

THEFT

6 Letters
STREWN
UPBEAT

7 Letters
ANYMORE

DELILAH
NEGLECT
ONSTAGE
OREGANO
OUTYELL
SCARIER
TRENTON

3 Letters
ADA
CAR
CHE
EGG
ELL
ITS
KEY
NET
ODD
OPT
PIA
RAE
RAM
REO

4 Letters
ABET
ALAN
ARLO

ASIA
CAME
CASS
CLAD
DEED
DODO
EPIC
ERLE
GRAB
HASH
HEAD
HOSE
IOTA
KENO
KIEV
KNOT
MYTH
NILE
NOPE
OTIS
PIED
RENO
RYAN
SASS

SHAM
SIRE
SPED
STAT
TACT
TAPE
TEST

5 Letters
ADAGE
ADMEN
ASHEN
AWARD
DELHI
ENTER
HONEY
IDAHO
LARGO ✓
LEERY
MAINE
MEARA
NEPAL
NIGHT
PACER

5 Letters	ESTHER	**7 Letters**
PORCH	INSANE	ARSENAL
SCALP	MARNIE	HACKSAW
SONAR	MONROE	HARVEST
TOKYO	ORALLY	
	TILLER	**8 Letters**
6 Letters		PLAYMATE
APIECE		RESPONSE
ERASER		

11

3 Letters

ANN
BEA
CUB
DAD
ERE
EVA
IMP
IRE
LIT
LOW
MIA
ODE
ONO
RAT
TAR
YEW

4 Letters

ACHE
ACRE
AJAR
ALMS
ARIA
AWAY
BRAT
ENVY
ERIE
EWER
FAIR
IONE
IRON
JOAN
KERN
KILO
LOIN
LORI
MAIN
NAPA
NEED
ONTO
PIPE
PITA
PLOY
REDD
SARI
SHOD
SNAG
TEND
TYNE
VAIN

5 Letters

ABBEY ✓
ADMIT
BOONE
CABIN
CLONE
CONAN
DREAD
DRIVE
ENEMY
ERODE
KENYA
MACAW
NEWEL
ORGAN
RENEE

RYDER	ERRING	TORONTO
TANYA	FASTEN	
UNTIE	LADDER	**8 Letters**
	NEATEN	CLARENCE
	YEARLY	ELEVATOR
6 Letters		ENORMITY
ATTEST		OVERTAKE
CREATE	**7 Letters**	
DREDGE	BICYCLE	

12

3 Letters
ALE
AMI
ART
DEL
DEN
ERR
EWE
NAM
OLE
RIP
TIE

4 Letters
ABED
ABEL
ABUT
ALAS
ALIT
ARCH

BRAG
DEMI
EDIT
ELAM
ELIA
ELLA
ERIN
ERMA
LIEN
LOBE
LOOT
LOSS
LOUT
METE
NEAP
OLEG
ONCE
PELE
PLED
RAGE
RIPE
ROLL
SEMI
SMUG

SODA ✓
TESS
URAL
VASE

5 Letters
AESOP
ALIAS
CACHE
CHILL
EAGER
FINAL
GLASS
GLEAM
HENIE
INEPT
LAYER
MORAL
OPERA
PANDA
REPLY
ROLLE
SLURP
TENTH

TINGE
USAGE

6 Letters
AFGHAN
ATTEND
CASHEW
NEVADA

7 Letters
BREATHE
DOGSLED
FORMULA
HATLESS
NEEDFUL
STEELER
TEENAGE

10 Letters
LETTER-
HEAD
PARLIA-
MENT

3 Letters
APE
BIN
BOA
DRY
LAD
LES
NIA
NIB
OPE
PEN
RID
SIC
TIA

4 Letters
ALDA
ALEC
ANTE
AVON
CLEO
DEEM
DEER
DISK
EDIE
FREE
FROG
GOLD
GORE
ICKY
INGE
LARD
LEST
LISA
LYRE
MAUI
NEIL
NOSE
ODOR
OTTO
OVAL
OXEN
PRAY
RANT
RATE
REAL
REBA
ROOF
SLED
TALC
TOGA
TRAM

5 Letters
AMISH
BASIC
ELLIE
EMERY
ENSUE
EXPEL
GEENA
IDEAL
INANE
NASTY
NEEDY
PORKY
RANDY ✓
SELMA

SINGE   LANDON   ORLANDO
TATER   SALAMI   RENEWAL
         SKATES   STARCHY

6 Letters   YELLOW

ARABIA
ARTIST   **8 Letters**
ERNEST   **7 Letters**   COSMETIC
FEDORA   FINICKY   FRANKLIN
         GENTEEL

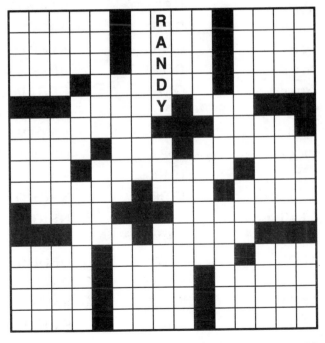

31

14

3 Letters

ABE
AGO
AMP
ARM
AWL ✓
BOG
DID
DUO
OHO
REN
REP
TEA
VIE

4 Letters

AIDA
ALOE
ANNE
ASEA
ATOP
BELA
BERN
CONK
DELE
EASE
ELLE
EVER
GEAR
GEEK
GLIB
GNAT
GOYA
GRID
GRIP
HAAS
IDEA
IDLE
ISLE
LOWE
MEET
MIST
MUSE
NULL
POSY
RODE
SADA
SELA
SHIM
STAN
TAME
TRIP

5 Letters

ARIES
AVERT
BRAVE
EDGAR
ELIOT
EMPTY
GROSS
HABIT
NACHO
NEIGH
OCEAN
ORONO
RALLY
RATIO
SMEAR

SNARE	ATTILA	SAHARA
TAHOE	BEANIE	WIRING
VADER	CHALET	
VERGE	CHARGE	**10 Letters**
	ENABLE	EISEN-
6 Letters	GROCER	HOWER
AHCHOO	HOMIER	HULLA-
APACHE	RETAIN	BALOO

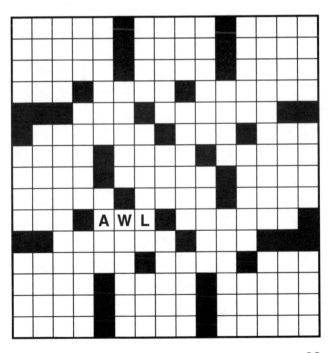

15

3 Letters
BIT
EGG
ELL
ENA
INN
ITT
LAS
RAN
REB
TAD
TAI

4 Letters
AFAR
AIDE
ALTO
ANNA
ARTE
AUDI

BEST
CELL
CHAN
EAVE
EDAM
ETON
ETTA
EVEN
GISH
GLEN
HARE
HOLD
INCA
INFO
LAUD
LINT
LONI
MOTH
NOTE
ODIE
OGRE
SCAR
SCAT
STAG

STET
STIR
SUIT
TAIL
TERI
TINA
TORE
WOOD

5 Letters
ANTON
EMEND
GIANT
GRILL
HINES
IDAHO
IDIOM
INERT ✓
INLET
IRISH
LATER
LEARN
LEECH
MINUS

	5 Letters	6 Letters		7 Letters
NAVAL		ENTREE		LARGEST
ORION		HOARSE		MISLEAD
SINAI		LENTIL		VASTEST
STONE		SALINE		
STOVE				8 Letters
TASTE		7 Letters		BEWILDER
TRAIT		GILLIAN		LAVENDER

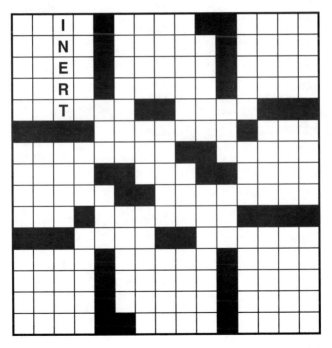

16

3 Digits

114
179
519
569
690
822
894
946

4 Digits

0114
0205
0418
0532
0859
0948
0975
1254
1732

1959
2016
2994
3010
3068
3173
3243
3299
3478
3878
3948
4071
4072
4188
4191
4380
4762
4988
5820
6425
7165
7294
7638
7979

7992
8047
8455
8627
9009
9359
9541

5 Digits

01712
03597
04338
17722
26421
29848
30902
39714
40587
56003
58549 ✓
78289
83365
83919
95452

96392	314387	8218177
97294	794660	8542179
		9013303

6 Digits **7 Digits**
102454 0787208 **8 Digits**
118122 1181850 16179353
215150 3257934 60148493
301297 4827100

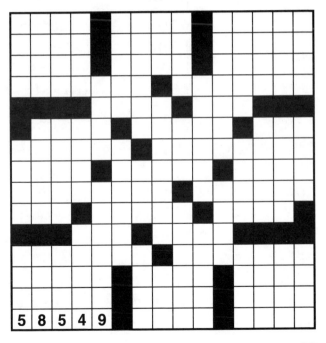

17

3 Letters
ADO
AWE
CAR
CEL
EON
ERR
FLU
LIL
NIT
RAH
TAT
UMA
YEN

4 Letters
ABED
ADAM
ALAN
ALEE

AMEN
AMOS
AXEL
BABA
BLOW
BOOT
CALL
CLEF
CREE
CROC
DERN
DIDI
ELKE
ERIC
EVAN
EVEL
EXAM
GENA
IVAN
LARA
LAVA
LEDA
LEER
MANY

MEMO
MOLE
NEVE
OREL
RAVI
STUD
TORI
URAL

5 Letters
ALVIN
ARENA
ATARI
BACON
CREST
DREAD
EGRET
LEWIS
LIBEL
LOWER
MAINE
NEATO
NERVE ✓
RELIT

SMELT	PROFIT	FULFILL
SPOKE	SEDATE	GALAHAD
	SNORED	ORGANIC
6 Letters	UPRISE	
ENOUGH		**8 Letters**
GLENDA	**7 Letters**	ODOMETER
IMPEDE	ALCOHOL	UMBRELLA
MISFIT	DIAMOND	

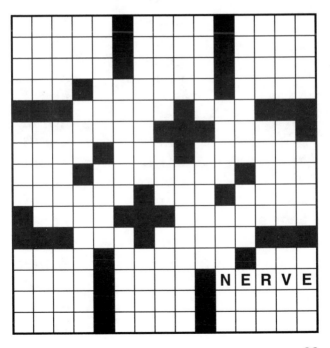

18

3 Letters
ACT
AYE
BUS
DEE
EMO
LEE
LEX
NIA
ORK
RAE
RAP
RAT
ROW

4 Letters
ABET
ABUT
ACNE
ACRE
AFRO

ARGO
ARIA
BAIO
BOLO
CALM
CALS
CANE
DEEP
EAST
EGAD
ELLA
EROS
ERST
IRIS
IRON
KEEL
LAHR
LANE
LORE
MAYO
MIRE
OBIE
ONYX
OPAL
ORAL

REAR
RITA
SALE
SEER
SETH
SIAM
SLOT
SNOW
TOOT
TREE
TROY
UPON

5 Letters
AGREE
ALERT
ATOLL
CLARA
ELOPE
ELROY
ERROL
ETHER
FLING
KEIRA
LUCAS

		5 Letters							

MARLA   THERE   **7 Letters**
METRO   TIDAL   STARLIT
NILES   WEIGH   STEINEM
RADIO   WHEAT
RAITT   **9 Letters**
RICER   **6 Letters**   GIBRALTAR
ROLLE   DETAIL   NECESSARY
ROPER ✓   TREBEK

19

3 Letters
AMY
ANT
BID
EEL
ERA
EYE
GAS
ONE
PER
PIT
WAD

4 Letters
ANKA
AUTO
AVON
BALI
BASE
COMO
DONE
EARP
EASY
EDIT
ESPY
ETNA
EURO
GRAM
HAAS
HASP
HOCK
HOLE
ICON
LANG
MUIR
NINA
OVER
PERT
PROF
PSST
ROAM
RUDE
SEMI
SLAB
SLOP
SPRY
TEAL
VOTE
WACO
WIRE

5 Letters
ALDER
ALLOY
AMISS
ANISE
APART
ARISE
BEERY
CLOAK
ELLEN
ELMER
EMERY ✓
ERICA
GENIE
HENIE
IRANI
KNIFE

5 Letters		
LOUPE	STEEL	HOOPLA
PASTA	UNTIL	IODINE
PECOS		NEVADA
PIPER	**6 Letters**	SHRIMP
REPOT	ASIMOV	
RERAN	ASSAIL	**8 Letters**
SHALT	AVALON	CARELESS
	BEWARE	MISSPENT

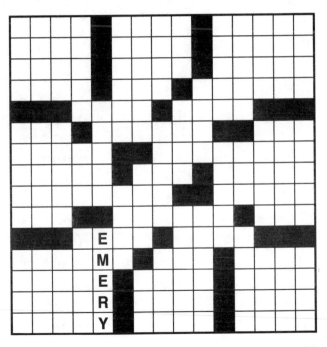

20

3 Letters
AID
AMI
ARK
ESS
FOG
HER
NAP
NEE
NOR
OAT
ORR
SIX

4 Letters
ALAS
ANTI
ARCH
ASEA
ASTI
AUNT
CLAW
DEAN
DEMI
DUET
ELLE
ELSE
ERIN
ERMA
ETTA
EYRE
HEFT
HEIR
IRAN
ITCH
LADD
LADY
LASH
LENS
MULE
NATE
NEWT
OLAF
OUST
PLIE
REAM
RULE
STAR
TARA
UNDO
YARD

5 Letters
AARON
ACTOR
APTER
ASPEN
DAMON ✓
EXIST
GREER
HINDU
MEARA
NEPAL
ONION
REMIT
SANTA
SPIEL
STOOL

TEPEE
TEPID
THANK
TINGE
TRUSS
UNIFY
VIOLA

6 Letters
ARGYLE
AVENUE
RATTAN
REPEAT

9 Letters
EYEOPENER

LIBRARIAN
PERSONNEL
REBELLION

10 Letters
IRRITATION
POINSETTIA

21

3 Letters
ALL
BAH
COT
EVE
EWE
FOE
IRE
LEA
NIB
ROE

4 Letters
ABEL
AIDA
ALUM
AREA
ARLO
CAME
CARR

DOLT
EARN
EDDY
EDGY
EDIE
EDNA
GLEE
HAVE
KELP
KITE
LANA
LOAD
NORA
OATH
ODOR
OSLO
SLAT
STIR
TEAR
TEEN
TEND
THAW
URGE
WASH

WATT
YEAR
YOWL

5 Letters
ABASH
ABOVE ✓
ADAMS
ANNUL
BLAST
BREAK
CARLA
COHAN
ERECT
LADLE
LAYER
MOVIE
NASTY
NEWEL
ONSET
REACT
RELIC
SCAMP
SHORT

THROW	PAROLE	EYEBROW
TRADE	SCORCH	RANCHER
	TATTOO	ROOFTOP
6 Letters	YANKEE	
APPEAR		**8 Letters**
ARMORY	**7 Letters**	DIAMETER
GANDHI	CLEANER	ULTERIOR
OILIER	DYNAMIC	

22

3 Letters

ARE
ELI
ELL
EVA
FAN
IDA
ILK
LIE
NET
SPA
STY
TEE
YAK
YAN ✓

4 Letters

ALDA
CADE
CENT
EATS
EDAM
EWAN
HERO
LAND
LASS
LATE
LAVA
NEAR
NEON
OMEN
PELE
RAID
REDO
SAGA
SELA
SKYE
SLAM
SLOB
SLOW
TEEM
TROD
ZERO

5 Letters

AIDAN
AISLE
ASIDE
AVERT
CATER
CREPE
DRAIN
EAGLE
ETHAN
FLICK
HYENA
INEPT
LAMAS
MANDY
NEATO
NOTCH
OFTEN
PARTY
PEALE
PLAIN
REEVE
REFER
SPRAT

STEVE	ONWARD	ELECTOR
TREAT	PENCIL	KWANZAA
VERNE	PESETA	LILLIAN
	REPORT	
6 Letters	WEALTH	**8 Letters**
ENDORA		BEWILDER
ERRAND	**7 Letters**	SEPARATE
KNOTTS	ASHTRAY	

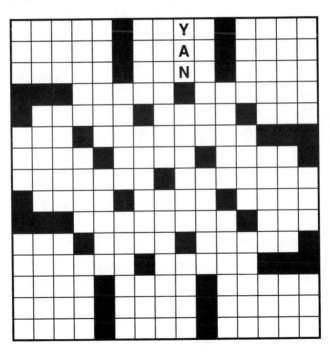

23

3 Letters
ADA
AHA
ALF
ALP
ARI
BIG
ELK
ERE
INA
LAS
LEE
PIG
REF
SAG
VAN
YIN

4 Letters
ACHE
AFAR
ALAN
ANDY
ANNE
COOL
ERLE
ERST
FAIR
GAFF
HIKE
HOLD
IDEA
INDY
LEAF
LEVI
LILT
LINK
MATE
MEET
NICE
ORAL
OTTO
OVAL
PARE
PAVE
POLL
RASH
RENE
TAOS
THEE
THEM
UNTO
UTAH

5 Letters
ACRID
ALIBI
ANITA
CHINA
FARCE
HINDI
INSET
LENIN
LUMPY
NILES
OPERA
PLEAT
SHEET ✓

TALON LATINO COASTER
VENUE PLIERS CONNORS
RONALD IRANIAN

6 Letters TACKLE
ATTACH
CANINE **8 Letters**
CLAIRE **7 Letters** POSITIVE
ITALIC AIRIEST RESTRAIN
ATTRACT

3 Letters
AVA
EMO
ERA
LAD
LAW
LIV
NOD
ONE
OWE
SAY
SHE
TON
TWO
YEA

4 Letters
ACNE
AMID
ANTE
ARIA
DEMO
DIDI
EMIT
EPIC
ERIE
FLEW
GLOP
ICON
ILIE
ITEM
KERR
LENT
LIMA
LIMO
LIRE
MAKO
MIRE
ODIE
ODIN
OPEN
OPIE
PACE
PEEL
PREP
RENT
RIND
RIOT
SALE
SIDE
SIGH
TEMP
TIRE
TITO
TOIL
TOTO ✓
YARN

5 Letters
AORTA
ATLAS
DRIVE
ELTON
EMPTY
ENDOW
FLAME
HENCE
IDIOM

5 Letters	6 Letters	
LEONA	**6 Letters**	VIOLET
MOTEL	CELERY	WADERS
NORTH	CENSOR	
RERAN	COMPLY	**8 Letters**
STAIR	ENTICE	AMERICAN
TALIA	LITCHI	EASTWARD
TWEED	OCELOT	ELEPHANT
		TELLTALE

25

3 Digits
064
096
197
442
457
545
594
680
883
967

4 Digits
0676
1431
1466
1646
1823
2086
2205

2300
2426
2464
3841
4245 ✓
4793
4828
5430
5474
5626
5926
6404
6451
6496
6517
6721
6991
7001
7294
7309
7451
7688
8844
9036

9145
9649
9724

5 Digits
01496
07267
16112
17538
38908
40438
41256
42140
43599
43709
43819
59939
60559
61086
63312
64911
65629
66114
66253

66467	**6 Digits**	**7 Digits**
67566	234492	6541419
73361	496393	8786911
87371	587846	
94991	690288	**8 Digits**
96472	713194	14673870
99626	946957	91351566

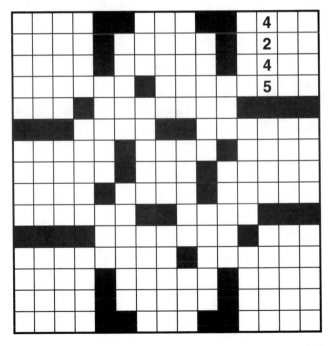

3 Letters

ATE
DIM
ESS
HUB
IRA
ITT
LED
LES
MIA
POL
WES

4 Letters

ALEE
ALEX
AMES
ARAB
ASEA
ASHE ✓

BASS
BING
CHAR
CLIP
DARK
DEPP
EASY
EAVE
ELIA
ELSE
ENID
ERIC
GARP
ILKA
KETT
KILN
LANE
LIST
MEOW
NAIL
NEAL
NEAT
NEIL
OLEG

OREL
PETE
PSST
RENO
SKIN
TARA
TART
TOGS
TUNA
WALT
WHIP
WICK

5 Letters

AGONY
CHAIR
DENIM
ETHIC
GENIE
HURON
ICING
KNUTE
NADER
OBAMA

PRISM
ROMEO
RURAL
SERUM
SLYLY
STALL
TRACK

6 Letters
ASHORE
POMPOM
SALINE
TYRANT

7 Letters
ANATOMY

DELILAH
PILLBOX
WHOEVER

8 Letters
INITIATE
TOLLGATE

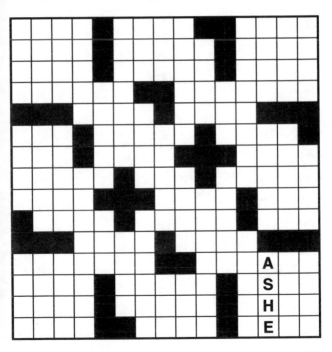

27

3 Letters

AMP
AND
BID
BOA
END
NIL
OHO
ORB
REB
ROE
RYE
SPA
TIM
WIN

4 Letters

ALMA
ALOE
ANTI
ASTA
ASTI
ATOM
BAIO
BALE
BETA
BRIE
CELT
CENT
CIAO
CLOT
DAVE
DYAN
ELSA
EMIR
ETNA
ETON
HOPE
HORN
ILSA
IRAN
LAIR
LANA
LISA
LOOP
MALL
MEAN
NINA ✓
OGLE
OMAR
PAPA
PIER
SCAR
SLAV
SOLE
TOTE
TRAP

5 Letters

AHEAD
ATARI
BASIS
DEBRA
DOBIE
EARLY
EMCEE
GLORY
IOWAN

LORRE	**6 Letters**	CONCERT
OCHER	ARCADE	NETTING
OCTET	CRAVEN	NIAGARA
PARIS	ERRAND	OBSERVE
SAGAN	IMPACT	
SCRAP		**8 Letters**
STING	**7 Letters**	CLERICAL
TOOTH	ADDRESS	OPERETTA

28

3 Letters

APE
ARE
EON
GNU
IMP
MIL
NUN
REV
SHY
URI
VEG

4 Letters

AHEM ✓
ALEC
AREA
ARTE
COST
CRAM
DANE
DIRE
DRAG
ELAM
ERLE
FAKE
FIDO
GASH
HERE
LIRA
LOIN
LULL
LYRE
MENU
MYTH
NAVY
NEAR
NOME
OHIO
OILY
OKRA
RAIL
RAKE
REAM
RITA
ROAR
SITE
STAN
STET
VASE
VINE
YOUR

5 Letters

ANWAR
AUGER
EDWIN
EVERY
GLENN
HENIE
IRATE
KEIRA
MEDIC
MERYL
MINEO
NEPAL
NIECE
ORATE

5 Letters		
ORION	TYLER	**7 Letters**
PEARL		EMERSON
RADAR	**6 Letters**	EMPEROR
RADIO	ATTACH	GLARING
RALPH	ENAMEL	HUNGARY
RETAG	GANDHI	PROGRAM
SLURP	SHOULD	

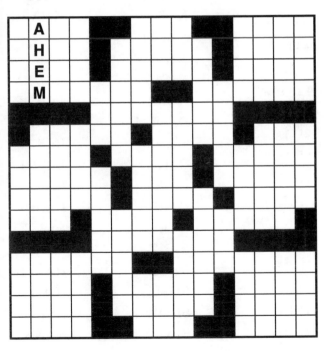

29

3 Letters
ADE
AIR
ILL
ITS
MEN
RAP

4 Letters
ABED
ALDA
ALVA
BOSS
DAHL
EDNA
ERST
FIRM
GALL
GEER
HERD
IDEA
ILIE
INGE
JIFF
JOHN
LAZE
LOLA
NAME
NARY
NEMO
NICE ✓
NIGH
NORA
ODIE
ODOR
OLGA
OMEN
OTIS
OVER
RANT
REED
ROME
SHOW
SIAM
SLOG
SNIT
SPRY
STUB
STUN
THUS
TORI
TWIG
WEAR

5 Letters
ACORN
ACTOR
ALERT
BASTE
BAYOU
BEERY
BLOOM
DIVER
ELLEN
HALVE
HOTEL
IRANI
NANNY

ORBIT	WILDE	**7 Letters**
ORSON	YOURS	ANDIRON
SENSE		FEDERAL
SILLS	**6 Letters**	ONSTAGE
START	LAZIER	
TAINT	OODLES	**8 Letters**
TRAIL		SARASOTA
UNDER		SCALLION

30

3 Letters
ALE
AWL
EMO
ERR
EWE
EYE
HEN
NIA
NIB
OAF
ONO
RIB

4 Letters
ARIA
ARID
AVON
BAWL
BOSC
BULB
BUST
EDEN
ELKE
ELLA
ELLY
ELMO
ERIE
FORK
HAAS
IDOL
INFO
LORI
MARC
MESA
METE
NASH
OKAY
OVAL
RILE
ROLL
SAME
SEEN
SHOE
SOFA
TEAM
TILE
TOLL
UNTO
URAL
WARN

5 Letters
ADORN
ASTRO
COINS
DEERE
EMBED
GARBO
HAITI
IDAHO
INLAY ✓
ISLET
LEONI
LOONY
NASTY
NEEDY
OLSEN

SEDER	**6 Letters**	STREEP
SHOOK	ASLEEP	TENNIS
SIREN	GALLEY	TRAVEL
TANYA	GIBSON	
VERSE	GOLDEN	**7 Letters**
YEARN	OREGON	ENHANCE
	ORIGIN	MARSHAL
	SHEENA	MELANIE

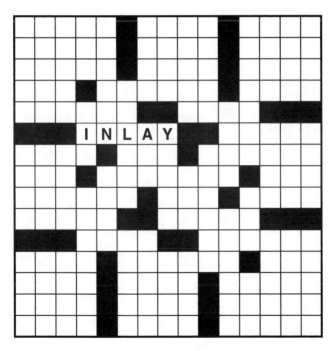

31

3 Letters

ANT
ARI
EGG
EGO
ELF
ERA
HAN
MAC
OWL
TAI ✓
VAT
WHO
YEA
YON

4 Letters

ALAS
ANNE
ASIA
ATOP
BOLO
CALL
COMO
DEER
EDIE
EDIT
HIND
HOAR
HYPE
KRIS
LENS
LIRE
MANE
MAUI
MOCK
MOON
NEAL
NINE
ODIN
OGRE
ONCE
OVEN
PITA
PLUM
PURR
SAKE
SPAM
SPUN
TEAL
TEAR
TENT
THAT
WRAP
YELL

5 Letters

AISLE
ASTER
AUDIE
BOISE
ELIOT
EPSOM
EVOKE
GEESE
GREET
HENNA
NACHO

OFTEN SMASH HYMNAL
OLIVE SPOOK IGNORE
ORDER TOTAL LEGEND
PASTA UNION NETHER
RANGE WHINE ROOKIE
REPOT   STOLEN
SARGE **6 Letters** SYSTEM
SEINE ERNEST

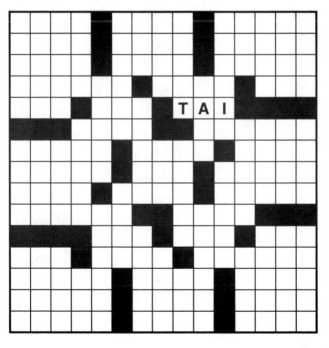

3 Letters

ABE
AFT
ATE
BED
ESS
EVE
LEI
LOU
POI
PRO
ROY
SIB ✓
TAT

4 Letters

ALMA
ARES
ASEA
ASTI

BALI
DARK
DEWY
ELSA
EROS
ETON
EVEL
HOST
IGOR
ILSA
ITEM
JEST
JOSE
OLAF
ORCA
PINK
REIN
SCAT
SEEP
SLEW
SLIM
SOAP
STIR
TAPE

TARA
VAMP
WAIT
WASP

5 Letters

ALVIN
AMISS
APPLE
APTER
BELLE
CARON
CESAR
CLOUD
ELATE
ELSIE
EVITA
GATOR
HOAGY
LEAVE
ORONO
PALER
RANDY
REBEL

SMITH	MELVYN	ENDORSE
STALL	OPTING	ESTELLE
	OSMOND	GARMENT
6 Letters		GENERAL
EASILY	**7 Letters**	HEROISM
HAWAII	ACCLAIM	LEEWARD
MARVEL	EARHART	PRANCER

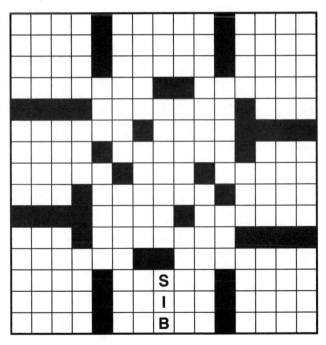

3 Letters
ADO
AND
ENA
IRA
LES
PEA
POE
RAM
REF
SHH
SKI
TAD
TAG

4 Letters
ABET
AREA
BIRD
BOAR
BOOT
BRAY
DIRE
EARL
EAST
ERIN
ERLE
ERMA
EWER
FLAT
FRAY
FUEL
GERE
GOAT
HARE
HOAX
IDES
IRON
ISLE
KILT
LIME
MENU
METS ✓
MORT
NAPA
OPIE
PEER
REND
ROSA
SELF
TAIL
TINY
TITO
TOLD
WEEP
YEAH

5 Letters
ALLAN
AWOKE
BRIBE
DROOL
EMOTE
FEAST
IRENE
KARAN
KNEEL
LATER

LENDL	ENABLE	WHITEN
NIGHT	HITTER	XANADU
RELIT	MARINA	
TEETH	NELSON	**7 Letters**
YEAST	OMELET	ASTOUND
	REALTY	ECONOMY
6 Letters	STEELE	ETHICAL
DELETE		KENNEDY

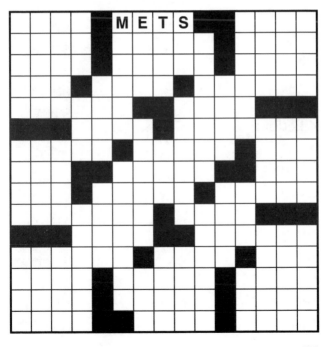

3 Letters

ASK
AWE
DEW
ERE
HUN
LOB
ONE
OPT

4 Letters

ALEX
ARGO
AVID
AXLE
CLAD
DELL
DILL
DINO
DRIP

EDAM
EDGY
EDNA
ELLE
ELSE
EMIT
EVEN
GOBI
ICON
INGA
INGE
IRIS
LINE
LOCO
MOOD
NEED
NEST
OBOE
OGLE
OLEG
OMAR
OPAL
OREL
OSLO

PANG
PESO
PEST
POEM
POGO ✓
POSE
REEK
RIND
SCAD
SEEM
SOON
SPAR
SPOT
STEW
STYE
TOOK
WELL
YAWN
YODA

5 Letters

ABATE
ALERT
ANGLE

DEGAS
EDDIE
HEAVE
KOREA
PEALE
PROBE
RENEW

RHODA
SCENE
SHORT
SOLAR
SPORT
TALON
TONAL
UNTIL

VITAL
YODEL

7 Letters
CANASTA
EYEBALL
GORILLA
ISOLATE

3 Letters
ACE
ALE
DEE
ELI
ICY
ROD
SHE
STU
TEE
TIC

4 Letters
ACME
ALIT
ANTI
ARCH
BIDE
DELI
EDEN ✓

EDGE
ENOS
ERIE
FESS
FILM
GRAY
HIVE
IOTA
IRAN
JEDI
LILT
LIRA
MEIR
NAME
ODIE
POOH
RICE
SARI
SECT
SHAW
STAR
TEEN
TELL
TERN

TRIP
TYPE
WHAT

5 Letters
ADANO
ASIDE
AVOID
AWASH
DIANA
DITTY
ELTON
ENACT
GRASS
HINDU
JESSE
OMAHA
RELAY
ROWAN
SANTA
SHREK
SKIMP
SNARE
SNOUT

SONIC   LAUDER   ELEVATE

STATE   OCTAVE

YIELD   PASTEL   **8 Letters**

           TAHITI   ALPHABET

6 Letters   WEASEL   HERITAGE

CORSET   IGNORANT

DREDGE   **7 Letters**   WESTERLY

EILEEN   CHARITY

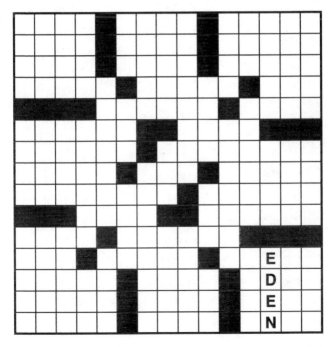

3 Letters
APT
EAT
EMO
GAB
LIV
MAC
RAG
RUE
TIN
YET

4 Letters
ALGA
ALSO
ARIA
BAER
BYTE
CLOP
CROC

DASH
DEAL
DIET
EAVE
ECHO
ELAM
ELIA
ETCH
FAME
FRET
GLEN
HERE
IDEA
IDLE
INCA
IVAN
KETT
LANE
LEER
LISP
LONI
MASS
MELD
MEMO

NICE
OMEN
PLOY
RINK
TERM
TILL
VETS

5 Letters
ARTIE
ATARI
BLOAT
ETHEL
GRAZE
GROUP
INGOT
IRANI
LAPEL
MARTY
MECCA
NIECE
OOMPH
OVERT
OZONE ✓

RABID	GROOVE	**7 Letters**
REPOT	INSEAM	ATTRACT
TIGHT	KARATE	OSTRICH
	NATURE	
6 Letters	OCTOPI	**8 Letters**
ATTACK	OFFEND	PREMIERE
COMBAT	OILERS	TREASURE
GRILLE		

37

3 Digits

158
197
320
361
420
687
692
737
799
821
967

4 Digits

0225
0336
0572
0814
1273
1567
1888

2145
2183
2407
2451
2596
2647
2986
3060
3169
3429
3444
3647
3732
3923
4004
4056
5279
5460
5821
5886
6051
6366
6818
6837

6974
7100
7199
7423
7603
8619
8701
9276
9389
9415
9448
9499
9534
9828
9890

5 Digits

08608
15892
17868
19931
22307 ✓
22870
29323

35654	69801	151987
38803	93291	195544
40869	96675	724513
47935	96891	970202
51884		
54325	**6 Digits**	**7 Digits**
63374	020585	3271500
63823	034623	6162808

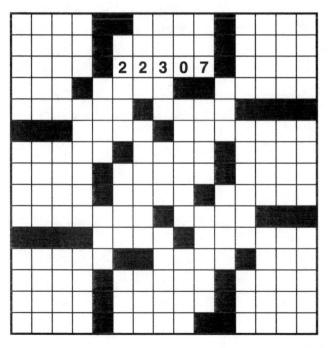

3 Letters
ASP
ATE
ERR
EVA
IDA
LEO
MET
NIT
RIP
RUN
TAG
TOM

4 Letters
AMES
ASHE
CLAN
CREE
DAIS

ELLA
ERLE
ETON
ETTA
FLAT
FLEA
GNAT
HOLE
IDOL
IFFY
LEST
LIEN
LIES
LIMB
LOGO
LOIS
LONE
NEAL
NERO
NOUN
OPEN
OTTO
SEEP
STUD

SWAP
TALE
TATE
TONI
TUNE
WINE
YALE

5 Letters
ANDES ✓
ASTIR
AUDIO
DEERE
EBERT
EMCEE
ERASE
INDEX
LOSER
NORSE
RALPH
SPELL
THREE
TORTE
UNGER

VIXEN

6 Letters
ENDIVE
ORIENT

7 Letters
BELIEVE

GROOMER

INGROWN

ISRAELI

ORLANDO

OVERSEE

REALTOR

RIVIERA

10 Letters
DELIBERATE

DRAWSTRING

IMPORTANCE

RINGMASTER

3 Letters

ALI
AMI
ASH
DAD
EEK
ERA
NET
PAT
REO
UTE

4 Letters

ABLE
AHEM
AIDE
ALEE
ALMS
AMEN
CHAD

DEER
DESK
EARN
EDAM
EDIE
ETNA
EVER
FISH
FLAP
GARB
GLOP
GOAL ✓
GREG
ITEM
KNEE
LAVA
LEAR
LEDA
LEEK
MEAL
MESA
NOME
OBOE
ODIN

OVER
RAVE
SADA
SELL
SILL

5 Letters

ANNIE
ASTER
BLANC
BRUCE
DRESS
EATER
EERIE
ENTER
HESSE
ILIAD
IVORY
LASSO
LEASE
LUNAR
OASIS
OTHER
PIETA

ROAST	**6 Letters**	ATHLETE
RULER	GANDHI	SERIOUS
SPARE	SUPERB	VERDICT
STALK		
THERE	**7 Letters**	**8 Letters**
UNITE	AMERICA	CRESCENT
UPSET	ANALYST	SCHEIDER
	APELIKE	

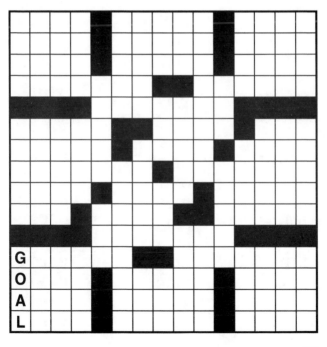

40

3 Letters
BED
BUS
EYE
ICY
ITT
RAE
REN
SKI
TOE
UMA

4 Letters
AGOG
AIDA
ALIT
ALOE
ARID
ARTE
AVON
AXLE
CAVE
EARL
EDEN
ELLE
ERIE
ESPY
GENE
ILIE
KATE
KEEN
LILI
LISA
MASK
MOST
NILE
NOSH
ORCA
OXEN
PANG
PERU
PLED
RILE ✓
RISE
SAGA
SANK
SCAR
SHUE
STAT
TICK
VEER
VILE
YEAR

5 Letters
ADANO
ALAMO
ASCOT
ATOLL
CIVIL
CURIO
EASEL
LEARN
LORNE
OSCAR
PHASE
RAITT
REMIT
RENEE
ROGER

SINAI
SNARE

7 Letters
AUSTERE
SEVENTH
THERAPY

TOUCH-
DOWN

6 Letters
EMERGE
ENDURE
HILARY
IGNITE

9 Letters
ORCHESTRA

10 Letters
COPPER-
HEAD
HEAD-
WAITER

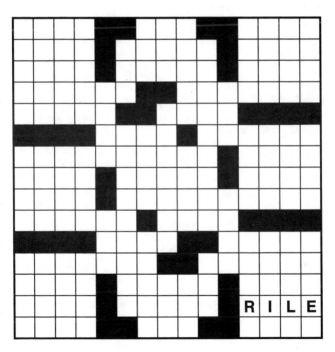

41

3 Letters

AIL
AIM
DID
EBB
GAS
HAM
HIT
IRE
ITS
LAG
MOO
PAW
ROE
ROO
SON
TEE

4 Letters

ACHE
ACRE
ANTI
CAAN
CHET
CITE
COEN
CRAG
EMIR
EWER
FAIR
FARM
GOAT
GONE
INCA
INDY
INGA
IOTA
LEER
MAKO
MINI
NEAT
NEON
NONE
NOTE
ODOR
OPAL
REST
ROOM
TRIM

5 Letters

ADAMS
AORTA ✓
ATARI
BLAKE
CHIRP
EDITH
ELECT
FROST
IDAHO
IDEAL
ORGAN
PRIME
REGAL
RERAN
RIATA
RIDER
STAID

TALLY

6 Letters
FACTOR
ROMPER
SAILOR
SEAMAN

7 Letters
ANNETTE
ATTEMPT
CAYENNE
CRYBABY
DEFENSE
LIBERAL

ORDERLY
TOEHOLD

8 Letters
DOMESTIC
FEARSOME
RETAILER
TRILLION

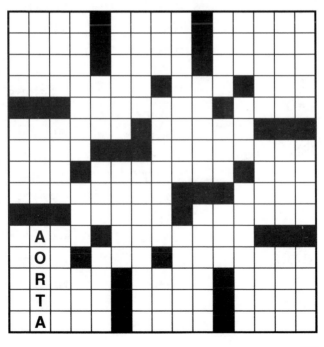

3 Letters

CRY
EAT
EMO
HER
HOE
LAS
LEG
OLD
RAD
SET
TIM
YES

4 Letters

ADAM
ALDO
ANTE
ARIA
ASEA
ASIA
BELL
BEND
COOP
CRAM
ECHO
ELAM
EROS
EYRE
HAVE
IONE
LAMP
LEAD
LIAM
MALL
MALT
MEET
NEMO
OLGA
OMEN
ORAL
OVAL
PAIL
PARE
POLO
RASH
REDO
ROAM
ROAR
ROSE
THIS
TYPO
WRAP
YELL
YORE

5 Letters

ABBEY
ABLER
ALERT
ANISE
ASPEN
ASSET
BEERY
BLAND
ELENA
ELSIE
ERNIE

5 Letters		
LEASH	RYDER	ELAINE
LOYAL	SARAN	GROOVE
NADER	TEPID	REVEAL
OBAMA	WRONG	
OTTER	YEAST	**7 Letters**
PEALE ✓		ASHTRAY
REPOT	**6 Letters**	TADPOLE
RETAG	ALLEGE	

3 Letters

ALE
AMY
ATE
BIB
EEL
END
INA
LEE
MIA
NAH
ORE
POI
VIA
WED

4 Letters

ACME
AMID
AREA
ARMY
ASTA
AXEL
BASK
BEER
BEVY
CALS
CANE
CARA
CLEF
ELLA
ELSE
EWAN
EXAM
EZRA
FEET
GALA
HYPE
IDLE
LEAN
LEAP
LENA
LOAF
MYNA

OMAR
OOZE
RARE ✓
REAM
REEL
SIAM
WACO

5 Letters

ABIDE
AERIE
AISLE
ARENA
EVADE
GRAMP
IDIOM
LAKER
LAMAS
MESSY
MOORE
NASAL
NAVAL
OATER
ONSET

OPRAH
ORION
TOTEM
VIDEO
VIOLA

BUDDHA
CORNEA
NONFAT
ORDEAL
OVERDO
PESETA
TILLER

UNISON
WELLES

7 Letters
APOSTLE
AVOCADO
PLIABLE
SALTINE

6 Letters
ARNOLD

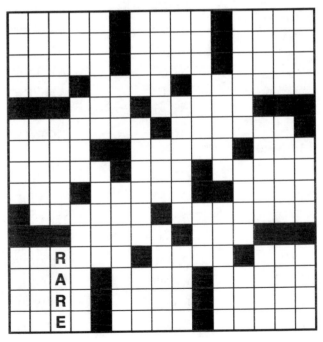

44

3 Letters
ADE
GNU
HEN
KEY
NIT
ONO
OWL
SAP
URN

4 Letters
ALGA
AMOS
ANNA
ARLO
CRIB
DARK
DINO
EDIT

ELIA
ENID ✓
FLED
HAIR
IDEA
IDOL
LEIA
LOCO
LORE
LUCY
MEEK
NEST
NOEL
ODIE
ODIN
OILY
OLDS
ONYX
PELE
PITA
POOH
RANT
REAL
SCAN

SEER
SIGH
SLOG
TIER
TORE
TREE
WINE
WOOL

5 Letters
ABYSS
ALONE
ANGER
ASKEW
BORIC
CLARA
CROOK
ELATE
HELLO
HERON
IRONY
LOOSE
NEWEL
NOHOW

5 Letters		
ROMAN	ANYONE	TSETSE
SENSE	BESTOW	XANADU
SHAFT	DOCILE	
SHARI	ERASER	**7 Letters**
TONER	PARLOR	DENTIST
	STAPLE	LITERAL
6 Letters	TENANT	POMPEII
ANKLET		WEIGHTY

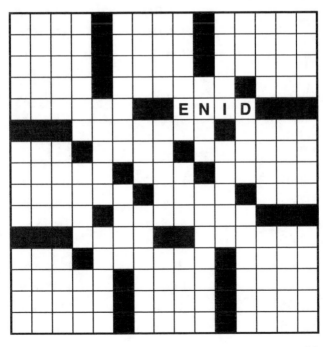

45

3 Letters

AGE
ALI
ELF
ERE
EVE ✓
GYM
KEG
LIL
MOB
TIE

4 Letters

ALEE
ARGO
AUTO
BLAB
CHAD
CLEO
DEEP
ECRU
EDDY
EGAD
ELLE
EVAN
FOND
GISH
HERE
HERO
ICON
IGOR
IRAN
ISLE
JADA
LEST
LEVI
LONG
LOON
LULU
OVER
PING
PORK
RITE
RODE
SLIM
STAG
TAIL
TENT
TONI
URGE
VOID

5 Letters

ABOVE
ACTOR
BROTH
CHURN
CURLY
DRAPE
EMEND
IGLOO
INERT
JESSE
LAUGH
LEARN
LODEN
MELEE
NEATO

NYLON	SEOUL	SOPHIA
OLIVE	TROOP	STRONG
PAPER		
REESE	**6 Letters**	**8 Letters**
RENEE	CANCAN	CARNEGIE
REVUE	ITALIC	ESCALATE
SEINE	RIBBON	RINGLING
	ROMERO	SABOTAGE

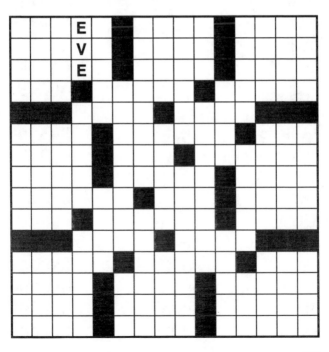

46

3 Letters
ABE
ARE
GEM
LAM
OAF
OUT
ROD
VET

4 Letters
AFAR
AMES
ANEW
ANKA
ANTI
ASTI
BETA
DRAT
EARN

EASE
EAST
EDEN
EDIE
ERIN
ETNA ✓
ETON
EVEL
EVEN
EVER
GAIN
GENT
HALT
KATE
LORI
MINI
NAME
NORA
ONTO
PERI
RAKE
REAP
REST
RHEA

RISK
SMOG
STAT
THAN
TINA
TINE
TOSS
TRIM
VERB

5 Letters
ADANO
BAGEL
BOARD
CEDER
DRILL
EBSEN
ELECT
ERODE
ERROR
GARBO
GEESE
HELEN

ITALY	VOTER	**7 Letters**
LEAPT	WROTE	EARSHOT
MIAMI		ENTREAT
ONION	**6 Letters**	LINEMAN
OPERA	LADDER	TUITION
SARAH	NUTMEG	VERANDA
SLATE	STRUNG	VOYAGER
TRIBE	TREMOR	

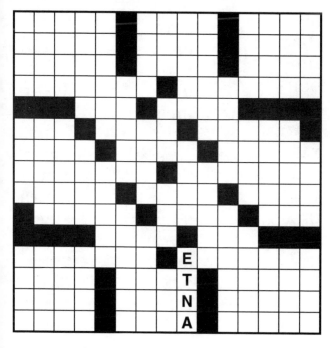

47

3 Letters
ARK
FED
FLO
FOR
LIV
MEL
MID
OOH
SIB
SOW
TAI
TAR
TSK
UMA
URI
UTE

4 Letters
AHEM
AHOY
ALIT ✓
ARES
ARIA
ATOM
AURA
DOLE
DONE
DRUM
EATS
EDNA
FOIL
HEFT
IDES
ITEM
LASS
LESS
LOVE
NAPA
NOSE
NUDE
OVEN
PSST
RAIL
SALT
SHUE
SOWN
TIME
TONE
TOTO
TYNE
WAKE
WIRE

5 Letters
ADULT
AVAST
DETER
DRIER
DRIFT
DWELL
EARTH
ERICA
ERUPT
EVITA
GAMUT
LATHE
LIBEL

MUSIC	TWICE	RELISH
NADER	WORSE	SERIAL
SELMA		
SHOOK	**6 Letters**	**7 Letters**
SOUPY	EFFORT	ETERNAL
SWIPE	ESTEEM	ETHICAL
TENSE	OLIVIA	GENTEEL
	PASTRY	MEMENTO

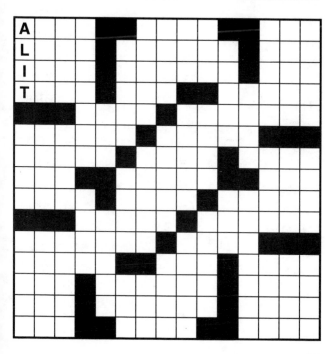

48

3 Letters

COP
ELL
EMO
ERR
LAB
MOE
NEE
ODE
SHY
USE
YES

4 Letters

ABBE
AFRO
AHAB
ALAN
ALOE
ASIA
BALE

BRAG
CAMP
CLIP
ENOS
EROS
GAVE
GLIB
HAYS
ILSA
IRIS
IRON
IVES
KONG
LANA
LEER
NONE
OBOE
OPAL
OPEN
OTTO
PEST
POUT
SALE
UGLY

URAL
UTAH
VAMP
WEAR
YARN

5 Letters

ABOUT
ALERT
ANTON
APART
APTER
ASKER
BAKER
CELLO ✓
DOUSE
EDGAR
GOOSE
HINES
HONOR
MOUSE
NAVAL
NOLAN
NOMAD

PETER	CORNEA	STANCE
RABBI	DARKER	WIGWAM
SCENE	DECEIT	
YEAST	ICEMAN	**10 Letters**
	REAPER	AFTER-
6 Letters	SEESAW	SHAVE
ARCHIE	SLATER	VETERI-
ATTAIN	SLYEST	NARY

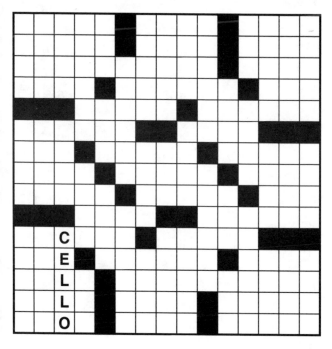

49

3 Digits

165
254
548
586
620
646
815
876
970
982

4 Digits

0236
0238
0366
0623
0720
0976
1347

1609
1633
2356
2678
2802
2825
3068
3160
3383
3643
4184
4623
4628
4724
4809
5436
5963
6482
6617
6618
7356
7615
7630
7656

8237
8626
8697
8769
8774
8980
9148
9207
9805

5 Digits

02700
06046
09404
10266
12961
17279
27254
27948 ✓
34199
42790
42940
51128
52484

61492	491106	848608
85486	642021	980555
98115	735219	

6 Digits

824885

7 Digits

102032	836428	2045883
395906	840306	3172049
432688	840386	4568611
		6203102

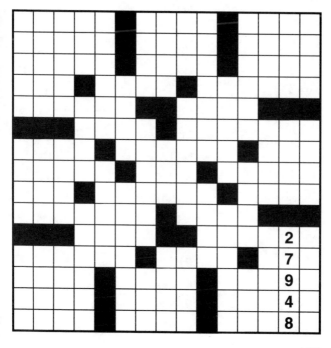

50

3 Letters

AID
ALE
DUO
ION
LEE
MAC
OLE
RAM
RED
RIO

4 Letters

AMOS
ANNE
ARTE
ASEA
ASHE
AWAY
BEEP

CASH
ELLA
ENVY
ERIC
ETCH
EURO
EWAN
GEAR
HERE
HONE
ITCH ✓
LEFT
LOGO
MAMA
MERV
MOAN
NATE
NECK
NICK
OLAF
PEEN
PEKE
PINK
POOR

RACY
RENT
SEEN
SHAG
SLEW
SPAN
STAN
SWIT
TUNE

5 Letters

ADOBE
ANGLE
ARDEN
ASNER
DOLLY
EAGLE
EASEL
EMERY
FELLA
FLARE
LABEL
LAYER
LYNDA

RULER
TROLL
WONKA

6 Letters
APACHE
ARREST
BANANA

CAGNEY
ELAPSE
HANDLE
HEAVEN
KERNEL
MANAGE
NESTLE

REVOLT
REWARD

7 Letters
ANYMORE
ARGYLES
ELEANOR
TREADLE

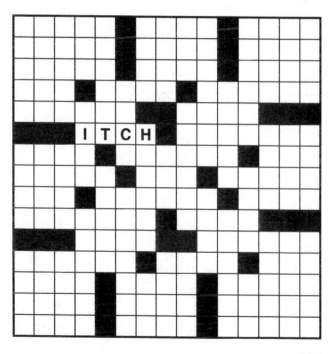

51

3 Letters

ACE
ALI
ARM
CAD
EBB
EVA
HAH
IDA
IRE
LEX
MAY
NET
ORR
RID
SIN
SPA

4 Letters

ACHE
ACNE
AIDE
ALEC
ALEE
ANEW
AXLE
BRAY
CAAN
EARP
ECHO
EDEN
ERIN
EVEN
ICON
IDOL
LEVY
MALL ✓
MAYA
MAYO
MEAN
MESA
NEIL
NILE
NOSY
OMEN
OOZE
OREL
OVAL
PEAT
RAVI
RELY
RHEA
RYAN
SANE
SASS
SELA
STEM
TEEN
THEE
THIS
TRAY
VEST
ZONE

5 Letters

ADLAI
ARBOR
ATTIC

DEBIT	**6 Letters**	**7 Letters**
DRYER	ADMIRE	ALMANAC
EATER	ELICIT	DENTIST
INDIA	HARASS	MIDTOWN
MOLAR	INHALE	MONARCH
NINNY	MARLON	PATTERN
SABLE	NORMAL	
YIELD		

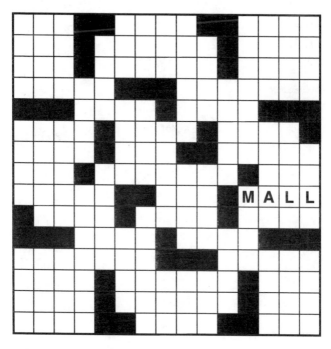

52

3 Letters
ADE
ASH
CHE
GAG
HAM
ORB
OWE
REA
TAR
WAS

4 Letters
AFAR
AHOY
ALAS
ANKA
ANTI
APEX
ARIA ✓

CHEF
EARL
EXIT
EXPO
HALL
HISS
IRAN
KAYE
LEIF
LILI
LOWE
NAIL
NELL
NOON
ODIN
ONYX
RASH
SITE
SPAT
TOLD
TONY
TREE
WISP

5 Letters
ADORN
AGILE
ANGER
BAGEL
BERET
CAIRO
CHANT
ELTON
EVITA
FLING
GREAT
HANOI
INDEX
LAHTI
MACHO
MOTTO
ORGAN
PATTY
PSHAW
READY
REFER
RILEY
SALAD

SEDER EATING RELATE

THEME EXEMPT

WALES FOREST **7 Letters**

MARINO ARABIAN

6 Letters NYLONS ELATION

AGASSI OCTOPI OBSERVE

EASIER REBATE ORIOLES

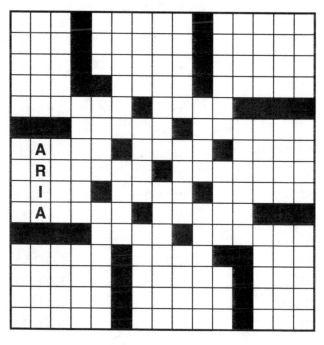

3 Letters

COO
DEW ✓
DON
ERE
HOE
LIT
RUB
SIR
UMP

4 Letters

ABEL
ACRE
AHEM
ARAB
AVOW
BELA
CEDE
ECRU

ERLE
EWER
FALL
FIFE
GISH
GRIP
IDES
IGOR
IRON
LATE
LEAN
LILO
LISP
MOON
PINS
POND
PONE
POPE
PRAY
RANT
RARE
REED
ROAN
SALE

SCOW
SODA
STUN
TEMP
UNIT
URAL
VANE
VOID

5 Letters

AERIE
AGAIN
ALFIE
APRON
BLEND
BREED
DAVIS
DWELL
ELMER
EVADE
LODEN
LOTTO
RAISE
RHODA

5 Letters	6 Letters	7 Letters
SILLS	DERAIL	ATLANTA
VILLA	OCCULT	EASTERN
YEAST	PARODY	ELDERLY
	PIGEON	HARDTOP
6 Letters	RAISIN	SNORKEL
AFFIRM	SKATER	VASTEST
AROUND	WEIGHT	
CAVETT		

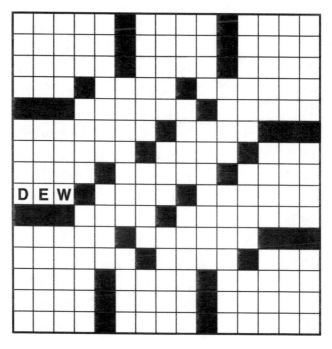

3 Letters

ADD
AMP ✓
AMY
DOC
DUB
GAD
GEM
LOY
THY
VIE

4 Letters

ALOE
ANDY
ANTE
ARID
ARLO
ASIA
AVID

BRAD
DESI
DIOR
EDDY
EMMA
GAFF
GAME
ILSA
ISLE
LEEK
LIMA
LOLL
MANY
MINI
NEAL
NERO
NEVE
OGLE
OKRA
OPEN
OSLO
PAIR
PEAL
ROAM

SIRE
TALK
TEAL
UNDO
WAIT

5 Letters

ABASH
ABNER
AIDAN
EGRET
EMEND
ESTEE
FLAIR
FLOOD
GRETA
INANE
INERT
JANET
JAUNT
METRO
NAIVE
NEATO
OASIS

OTTER	**6 Letters**	NUMERAL
PIANO	DILUTE	STETSON
RESET	ENDORA	TAFFETA
SARGE	FORCES	TENSION
UNITY	STATUE	TREETOP
YUKON		WILLIAM
	7 Letters	
	FONDEST	

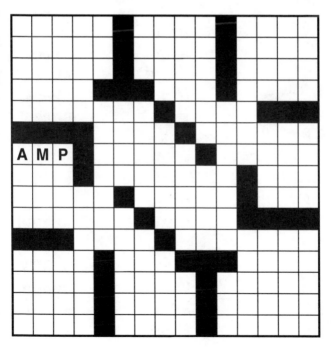

55

3 Letters
ADA
AID
BAH
BEA
CAW
DRY
FAR
GAM
HEX
LEI
NEW
OAT
OPT
ROW ✓
TOE
YUL

4 Letters
ALIT

AMMO
BASS
CELT
CREE
DELE
EMIR
ENID
ERIC
ETCH
HAIR
HILT
HONE
IONE
IVAN
LORI
MARE
OBIE
ODOR
OPAL
ORAL
PAST
PAVE
PIER
PLED

RILE
SILO
SLED
SNOW
STEP
STEW
TELL
TENT
TERN

5 Letters
ALOFT
APPLE
BERTH
CATER
CHESS
EMCEE
EXILE
HOMER
MCGEE
OPERA
ORSON
REMIT
ROOST

SINAI	CREWEL	DYNAMIC
SLOSH	METEOR	MILDEST
SMALL	RIDING	OUTYELL
STERN	TEAPOT	PROGRAM
TOWEL	TYCOON	RACEWAY

6 Letters **7 Letters** RUSTLER
AUSTIN DECIBEL TERRAIN

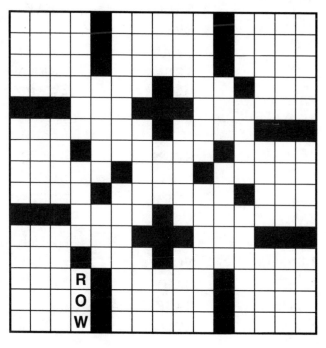

56

3 Letters

AWE
CAR
DAB
EAR
HEN
IKE
INA
JET
OAR
ONO
RAD
ROE
TAD
YAM

4 Letters

ABLE
ALAN
ALVA
AREA
DADA
DAME
DEEM
EACH
EBAY
EDIE
EDIT
ERIE
EVEL
EWAN
FETA
HARE
IDEA
JEFF
KEEN
KIEV
KNEW
NEST
NILE
NOSE ✓
OAHU
RAVE
RYAN

SHOE
TANG
TEST
TILE
TITO
TURN
VEND
VETS
WEAK

5 Letters

ARENA
AWARE
AWASH
BAMBI
BATES
DECOR
DELTA
DEMON
DETER
ENGEL
ERASE
EVICT
GABOR

5 Letters	6 Letters	WARREN
IRANI	DANDER	
MANIA	REALTY	**7 Letters**
RENEW	RINSER	ARMREST
SPOON	ROTATE	FLORIST
TALON	SINBAD	GIDDYAP
THANK	SYSTEM	NATASHA
VITAL	TATTER	

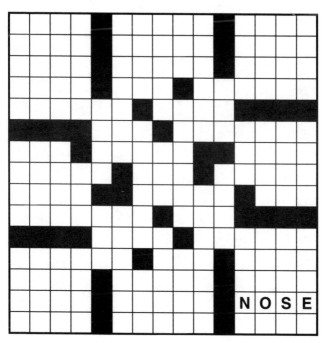

N O S E

57

3 Letters
ARE
ARM
ATE
BET
EGG
ELI
ENA
ESS
HEM
LEA
LET
OHO
PEA
SAL
VEE
WON

4 Letters
ALEE
ALSO
ANNE
ASEA
BOLO
BOSC
ELKE
ELSA
ERIN
EROS
ETTA
FAIR
FAME
GEER
GERE
GIVE
HAYS
HOST
MARK
MIMI
OREL
OUCH
OWEN
PERU
REEL
RENO ✓
SASH
SCAD
SEEN
SOUP
TAIL
TINE

5 Letters
AHEAD
ALIVE
ALTER
CAINE
DINER
DRAMA
EERIE
ERROR
IDLER
OILER
OLDIE
OMAHA
STEVE
UNSER

6 Letters

AMPERE
ANIMAL
ANTHEM
APPEAL
ARNESS
DAMSEL
DHARMA

ENERGY
ICEMAN
INMATE
REINER
REPEAL
SUITOR
UMPIRE

7 Letters

EMERSON
INDIANA
ONSHORE
ORCHARD
SESSION
TREMBLE

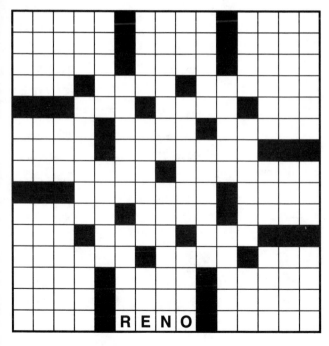

58

3 Letters

ANY
EGO
GAL
IRA
ITT
KEG
ONE
ORB
PER
REP

4 Letters

ACME
ADAM
ALAS
ALUM
APEX
ARES
ATOP

BUST
DECO ✓
DORY
ELAM
ELLA
ELMO
EPIC
ERLE
FLOE
GNAT
GREW
INCA
LOLA
MALT
MEMO
NAME
NELL
NOTE
PASS
REDO
ROLE
ROOT
SCOT
SELA

SILT
TAPE
UNIT
UNTO
URAL

5 Letters

ALLEN
ALONG
BROAD
DEGAS
DICER
ENOLA
ERODE
EXTRA
HONEY
KENYA
NINNY
NORMA
OATER
OFFER
RENEE
ROLLE
SALON

SCARE	**6 Letters**	CHICAGO
SONAR	FILLET	DEFRAUD
TEENY	FORMAT	LAYOVER
TOTEM	LAWMEN	MYSTIFY
VADER	PESETA	REFEREE
YODEL		TRACTOR
	7 Letters	
	ARABIAN	

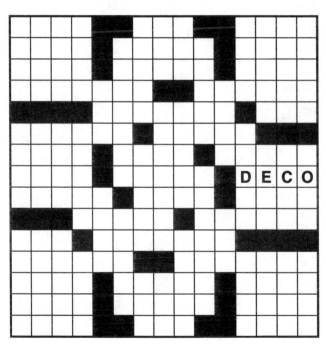

59

3 Letters

BEE
DEL
EVA
FRO
GAP
IDA
INN
ODE
RAN
TAG

4 Letters

ACHE
ALGA
AMEN
ASIA
CANE
COLA
EARN

ECRU
ERST
ETNA
EVAN
GARR
GIST
HILL ✓
ICON
KENT
LEIA
LIRE
MAMA
MENU
MITE
NINA
PAAR
PACT
PEEN
PEKE
RANT
RAUL
RIGG
ROAD
SEAM

SEMI
SKYE
SLUG
SOHO
SUIT
TALE
VAIN

5 Letters

ACRID
ALPHA
ASIDE
ATOLL
BOGIE
CIGAR
DANCE
ELATE
ELLEN
ENTER
ERICA
INANE
LEAFY
MICRO
MOUSE

PARIS	**6 Letters**	TAUGHT
REESE	ASLEEP	ZIPPER
RISEN	AZALEA	
ROYAL	GRUDGE	**7 Letters**
SASHA	OILCAN	ALASKAN
SERVE	ONLINE	CRUCIAL
TEMPO	POINTY	ILLEGAL
		UTENSIL

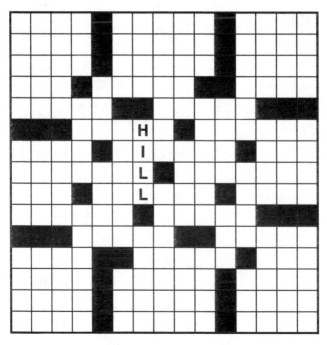

60

3 Letters

ERA
ERE
INK
OAT
OLE
PAL
POE
RAG
RIM
TIE
UNO

4 Letters

ALEC
ARIA
BAER
DELI
DINE
DRIP
EDAM
ELLE
GEAR
GONG
GRAB
HEDY
HOAR
HOLE
ILKA
ILSA
INGE
IONE
LANA
LION
MESA
NEAL
NORA
OBIE
ODIE
OINK
PEAR
PLIE ✓
RAIN
ROAM
ROBE
SAGA
SEER
SNAG
TOUR
YEAR

5 Letters

ALIAS
ARIEL
ASPEN
DITTO
ENEMY
HANOI
MERIT
MISER
OPERA
REGIS
RIATA
ROLLS
SLOPE
SOLAR
STRAP
TEMPT

TIARA	MADRAS	**7 Letters**
TWANG	REISER	APTNESS
TWINE	REMIND	DISMISS
	SIMMER	ETHICAL
	STREAK	IRKSOME
6 Letters	TREATY	PASTIME
EGGNOG		THINKER
EMERGE		

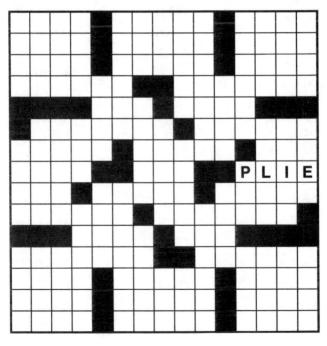

61

3 Letters

ANT
EEL
END
FAR
HAH
HAS
HIP
INA
NED
ONO
PAR
PUB
SAG

4 Letters

ALAN
ALDA
ALOE
AMID
AMOS
ANTI
BEAM
BOTH
DEAR
EDDY
EDEN
EZRA
HAIL
IGOR
ISLE
KETT
KNOT
LARK
LIEN
LIMO
MOLE
NEED
NOAH
ODOR
OLGA
OMEN
ONTO
OPAL
PINS
REIN
RITA
RYAN
SALE
SCAR
SHIP
TINA
TOLD ✓
UNDO

5 Letters

ABASE
ALAMO
ARRAY
ARTIE
BECKY
BENET
BOSOM
CINDY
EPSOM
FRIES
HEART
LINDA

MANIA	STALK	**6 Letters**
NOMAD	STRAY	AGASSI
OCTET	TARRY	BATTLE
OZONE	TEETH	HOOPLA
SKILL	TEPEE	RAISIN
SMILE	THINE	SKINNY
SNORT	TRADE	TEETER
SPARK		

62

3 Digits

047
130
240
335
337
389
526
532
700
741
882
888
912
946
954
975

4 Digits

0145
0336
0431
0907
1501
1560
1662
1769
2315
2612
2856
2955
3387
3590
3754
3872
4342
4409
5586
5671
6334
7530
7915
8254
8359
8362
8480
8740
8805
9257
9643
9778

5 Digits

00400
09744
11279
13154
22126
23475 ✓
38653
44118
44597
50784
52876
54713
65681
73617
79577

82151	**6 Digits**	**7 Digits**
93663	040787	1257451
94188	107807	1875449
94737	131058	5849383
98179	262659	6236877
98807	584520	7580537
98952	843161	8675542

63

3 Letters

ALI
AMI
CEE
ENA
ESS
GAS
IRA
KEN
LAP
RUM
YON

4 Letters

ACME
ACNE
ADAM
ALSO
ARTE
ASTA
CELT
CHAP
DALI
DISC
ENID
ERIE
ERIN
ERLE
EWER
FARR
HARP
HERB
IRON
MANN
MATS
MILK
MINE
NASH
NEMO
OBOE
OLAF
OMAR
OREL
PERU
PRIM
RAVI
RAYE
SEAN
SIRE
SORT ✓
SPAN
STAR
STAT
TAOS
UPON
URAL

5 Letters

ACTOR
ALICE
ALOUD
APACE
ASTRO
CELEB
GARBO
INSET
LAMAS
NASTY

NEPAL	WANED	MIDDAY
NOLAN	WILMA	NECTAR
OTHER	WORST	ONRUSH
REFER		PREFER
SEDER	**6 Letters**	REMOTE
SKEET	ASSERT	TRIPOD
STAIN	ATTACK	WEAPON
VOTER	LAWMAN	

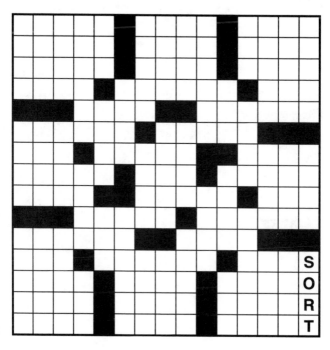

64

3 Letters

ARI
EON
GUY
IDA
IRK
MAA
NEW
OPT
OUR
STU
TEE
TOE

4 Letters

AGOG
AMEN
AREA
BELA
CITE
DOWN
EDIE
EDIT
EMIR
EMMA
ENOS
ERMA
FEEL
FLEW
FLIP
GALA
GENE
GLEE
HALE
IDOL
LANE
LANK
LIMA
LONI
MAYA
MICE
MIME
MIST
OGRE
OTTO
OVAL
PLAN
REAM
SAND
SAVE
SELF
SEMI
TEEN ✓
TEMP
TERM

5 Letters

ALOFT
ARENA
ELDER
ERASE
FLAKE
INERT
KERNS
LEIGH
LOREN
MELON
MIAMI

ONION	**6 Letters**	SUITOR
PAYER	AERIAL	TATTLE
PLEAT	ANYONE	
TEASE	BECAME	**7 Letters**
THROB	CONRAD	ASPHALT
WIRER	EASIER	DECIBEL
YIELD	ENTITY	PIANIST
		RECITAL

65

3 Letters

ALE
ATE
BEG
CUD
GAR
GNU
IMP
IRE
ITT
LEA
LIE
MIX
ONE
SHE
UMA
ZEE

4 Letters

ASEA
ASIA
ATOM
AVON
AVOW
BERT
CAST
DEAN
EAVE
EDAM
EYRE
HEAT
IDEA
IDLE
INGE
JAWS
LATE
LIZA
LUAU
MEND
MINX
MOAT
NERD
NEWT
NICK
OHIO
PRAY
RAKE
RAVE
RIDE
SECT
SWAN
TAKE
TIER
URGE
UTAH

5 Letters

ACUTE
AGREE
ARROW
ATARI
CUTER
EDDIE
ELENA
GLARE
IDAHO
JULIA
KEITH

NADER ✓

OATER

READY

RUMOR

SCANT

TEDDY

WATER

6 Letters

AIRMAN

CANCEL

IRONIC

LOCALE

NICOLE

ORIENT

SCENIC

SIGNER

7 Letters

CONNORS

DRAINED

EDUCATE

TOASTER

66

3 Letters

ADE
AFT
ASH
ASP
AYE
LIL
NAP
OWL
SAL
SEE
SKI
TIE
TRY

4 Letters

ALDA
ALEC
ALEE
ARES

ARIA
BEND
BOSS
CLAW
COAL
COVE
DEAL
ELLA
ELMO
EPIC
ERST
FELT
HERO
LAID
LUIS
LULU
NAPE
NERO
NINA
OPIE ✓
ORCA
REAL
REAR
SANE

SASH
SING
TAIL
TRUE
TYNE
TYPO
UPDO
WALL

5 Letters

AORTA
ARMOR
ASSET
BALSA
ELUDE
FRANK
LAURA
LINEN
LOONY
LOVES
LYNDA
NINNY
ONSET
OSCAR

		5 Letters			
OTTER		SNACK		BURLAP	
PEONY		STEEL		DEGREE	
RECUT		UNION		LIONEL	
RELIT		USUAL		NOODLE	
RERAN		WHOLE		RESULT	
RHINE				SPIRAL	
SCARF		**6 Letters**		STREAK	
SHORT		ANNUAL			

67

3 Letters

ALP ✓
CEL
EAT
EGO
INA
INN
LAG
MEL
NAM
WAX

4 Letters

AHAB
ALDO
ANKA
ANTE
BEEN
COIN
COST
DAWN
DOLE
DOSE
DRAT
ELAM
ELKE
ELLY
GAZE
HALO
HOLE
INCH
LAHR
LEDA
LEIF
LOST
LULL
NOTE
ODIE
ODOR
ONCE
OPAL
OPEN
OXEN
PAAR
PAWN
POET
RELY
RHEA
ROAM
ROAN
SADA
STUN
TROD
WANE
WELL

5 Letters

ADAMS
ALLOT
APPLE
CARON
CRIME
DISCO
EMEND
EMILY
HONOR
LEONI
MARCH

NYLON   TEETH   THREAD
OFTEN   TRACT   ZEALOT
RAOUL
RATIO   **6 Letters**   **7 Letters**
SHEET   ENAMEL   CONDONE
SITAR   GNAWER   ICELAND
SPREE   INGEST   NAUGHTY
               OPTION   SAINTLY

68

3 Letters

ARF
EGG
FIN
GIL
OLE ✓
OPE
ORE
OWE
OYL
PAM
ROE
SHY
TAB
TAM
VEG
VIM

4 Letters

AIDA
AKIN
ALIT
ALOE
AMMO
ARMY
BOAT
CAMP
CLAD
CLAM
DESI
DOFF
DOTE
ECHO
ELIA
ERIC
HARE
ILIE
ITCH
LENT
LIKE
LILI
LOPE
MASH
MESA
METE
MOTH
ORAL
OWEN
PEAR
PELT
PERT
STAR
SYNC
TYPE
YOKO

5 Letters

ABASE
ALIVE
ANITA
AROSE
CREEK
DEMUR
EBERT
ELITE
FLARE
LINER
LUCCI

OCHER	**6 Letters**	**7 Letters**
ORONO	BACALL	ADAPTER
RADAR	DOLLOP	BLOOPER
TITHE	FACIAL	ILLEGAL
VENUE	HYMNAL	OLYMPIC
WADER	IODINE	REMODEL
WAKEN	UNHOOK	TAILING

3 Letters

AGE
AHA
BAT
GAG
GOO
HER
HID
LEE
OAR
POT
RUE
SON

4 Letters

ACRE
AGOG
AMOS
ANNA
ARAB
AREA
ARGO
ASHE
BERN
BOLA
CORD
EAST
ENID
EROS
ETNA
EZRA
FORE
GILA
GRAB
GYRO
LARA
LOAF
LOIN
NEAP
NOAH
NOSE
NOSH
OOZE
ROAD

ROOM
SAIL
SOAR
SORE
SORT
TEAM
TRAP
UNDO
YANK

5 Letters

ADAPT
ADORE
AISLE
ALIAS
ALOOF
ARENA
BABEL
BADGE
BETTE
EBSEN
ENEMY
ENOLA
IGLOO

5 Letters		
ITALY	STANS ✓	ATTEND
KITTY	TALON	EDITOR
LEARN	TENSE	EMBLEM
ODDLY	TOOTH	IMPOSE
ORATE	TUTOR	LENTIL
PASTA		SOUGHT
REFER	**6 Letters**	UNBOLT
RINGO	ALUMNA	

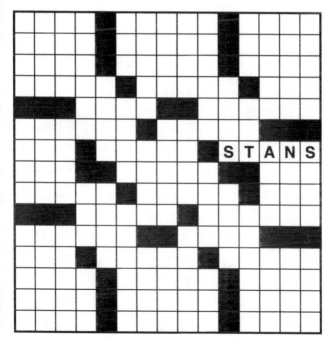

3 Letters

EAR
GAG
IRA
LAM
LES
NIT
OWE
RED
SAM
SEW
WOW

4 Letters

ABEL
AVON
BALI
BEET
CITY
DEAL

EARN
EBAY
EDAM
EMIT
ENID
ENOS
EROS
FALL
GNAW
IDEA
INGE
IOTA
IRON
IVAN
IVES
JANE
KONG
LANG
NEON
OMIT
OTTO
RASH
RIOT
RITE

SALE
SCAR
SEAR
SELA
SHIM
SILL
SOLO
STOP
TAPE
TEMP
WADE
WOOL

5 Letters

ADDER
AMIGO
ANITA
CABIN
COMIC
ELENA
ENGEL
ERICA
ERODE

FIELD	SANTA ✓	**6 Letters**
JOINT	SHONE	BIKINI
LEASE	SINGE	DREDGE
LEONA	STEER	ELICIT
NOLAN	TIMID	HECTOR
OLIVE	VALID	HYPHEN
OTTER	WAGER	TWELVE
RETAG	WAYNE	

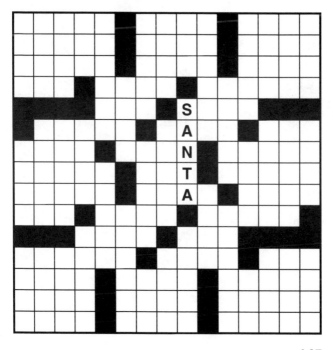

3 Letters

AHA
ANT
BED
BRR
DEB
EGO
EVA
ICE
ION
KEN
OAR
OHO
SAL ✓
SUN
VAT
VEE

4 Letters

ALDA
AREA
ARES
ARID
ARLO
BEAR
BEER
BONN
BURR
ELLE
ERIE
EVAN
FACT
GRAB
HEAR
ILIE
LIRA
LYRE
MESA
NODS
NOUN
OGLE
OTIS
OVER
RAUL
REBA
SASH
SENT
SIRE
SLAV
SODA
TACK
URGE
VETS
YVES
ZANE

5 Letters

ABODE
ADORN
ALOUD
ASTOR
ATOLL
BROIL
CLUNG
EASEL
IVORY
LAURA
LEDGE

OUTDO	BRUTAL	**7 Letters**
REEVE	ECLAIR	ATLANTA
SEDER	EDGING	CLARIFY
TEASE	LOWELL	GEORGIA
TENSE	MOZART	LEARNER
	STARER	RESTORE
6 Letters	WELDER	SELLERS
ARTIST		

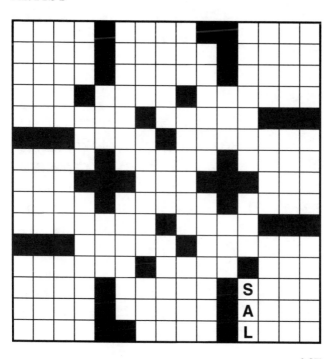

72

3 Letters

AGO
AIM
BRR
DEW
END
FLU
IMP
INA
IRE
LED
LEO ✓
RAM
TRY
WES

4 Letters

ALUM
ALVA
AMID
ARIA
CHAP
CLEF
DEER
EDIT
ELLE
ERMA
EWER
GRIM
HAIL
HAIR
HART
IRON
ISLE
KRIS
LACY
MEAL
MERE
NEAL
NOME
NOPE
PAAR
PLAN
RACE
REDO
RENE
RIDE
SHED
STET
TEST
THAI
TONI
YARN

5 Letters

ABIDE
ANNUL
AROMA
CAROB
DERBY
ERROR
GRAZE
HAREM
LIBRA
MOOSE
OCTET
PAGAN
RHINO

ROTOR
SHARI
STEED

6 Letters
ACCESS
CEMENT
HILARY

INVADE
NEEDLE
OWLISH
PLACID
RELENT
SPACEY
XANADU

7 Letters
BOOKLET
CHEETAH
ISRAELI
NATASHA
TEXTURE
ZEALOUS

73

3 Letters
ADA
AIL
ALL
DIN
EAT
EON
GIL
HEP
HON
LEG
OLE
RIB
RIO ✓
TIE
UMA

4 Letters
ALDO
ALOE
ASEA
BOOM
CARP
DADS
DIOR
ELIA
EMIR
ENOS
ERST
EVAN
GALE
IDOL
KELP
LEEK
LINE
LUAU
LUCE
MOVE
RARE
RINK
ROMP
ROSE
SEMI
SLOT
SOME
SOON
STEW
TINA
VAIL
VEER
VOTE
YELP

5 Letters
ADDER
BLAIR
GENIE
IDIOM
MELEE
MIAMI
NAOMI
NEIGH
PEARL
REACT
RELIT
SHAFT
SKULL

STUNG	HIATUS	**7 Letters**
TEASE	LONDON	AIRLINE
	MAYHEM	ERASURE
6 Letters	ONRUSH	FLORIST
ASIMOV	PLANER	LULLABY
ENRICH	POODLE	NEWSMAN
ERNEST	TENANT	RESTYLE

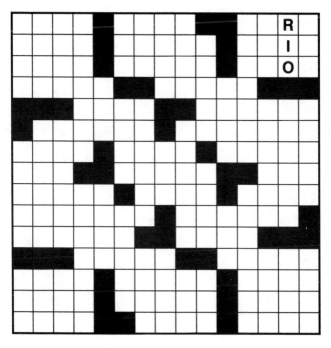

74

3 Letters

AHA
AVA
DAG
DEL
EWE
IRA
NET
OPE
TUX
UTE
WRY

4 Letters

ALTO
AMMO
ANNA
ARLO
AXEL ✓
BEAN

CAFE
CALS
DAWN
DECK
DIAL
EDGE
EDIE
EMMY
ERIC
ETNA
EYRE
GEER
GLEN
GOWN
HOBO
INGA
LAID
NEAT
NEON
NICE
ODIN
PAIR
PERI
PINE

PONG
PSST
RAIL
RASP
RICE
RYAN
SCAR
SING
SMUG
SORE
SOUP
THIN
THIS
TORE
WEPT
WING

5 Letters

ASIAN
ASTIR
BISON
DINER
DRAIN
ESSEX

HENIE	PIVOT	**6 Letters**
INDEX	SARGE	ALWAYS
IRATE	SHORE	AUSTIN
IRENE	SPRIG	ELAPSE
MAINE	STIFF	ICIEST
MOORE	TIBET	KNOTTS
MURAL	TWILL	RELIEF
NYLON		

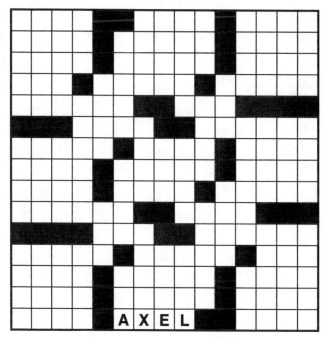

75

3 Letters

ARE
ASK
BRA
EEK
HEM
IDA
NAB
NOR
ONO
PEA
SHE
UMP
WIL

4 Letters

ABBY
AKIN
ALEE
ALGA
ALIT
ARAB
ASIA
COEN
CORE
DEAR
EARP
GALL
GISH
ICON
ILIE
INTO
ITEM
KILO
KNEW
LIAM
NEED
NOTE
NUMB
OKRA
PEON
PILE
PROM
RULE ✓
SCAN
SLUR
SNOW
SOLO
STUD
SWAM
TERI
TOLD
UPON
URGE
ZITI
ZONE

5 Letters

BUTTE
CAREW
CHORE
CORPS
EBERT
EERIE
ENOLA
ERNIE
KNEEL
LASSO

LATER	SPEND	ESKIMO
NADER	STANK	GANDER
OCCUR	UNDER	HANSEL
OCEAN	UPSET	IRONIC
OILER	YUKON	RESORT
OSCAR		REWARD
SEARS	**6 Letters**	SATEEN
SHAME	ENIGMA	

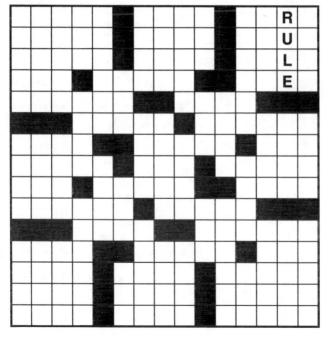

3 Letters

ACE
ALI
EAR ✓
ELI
ELM
FEW
GEM
ILK
ILL
KIN
LEI
NAN
PAC
RIM
SOD
TEN

4 Letters

ACRE

AIRS
ALAN
ASHE
BASS
BEER
CLAY
EDDY
EGAD
ERIK
ETCH
FACT
FATS
FINE
FLAG
FOOT
GENA
GENE
HEEL
HERD
ILSA
LADY
LILY
LIRE
MANE

NAIL
ODIE
OPIE
READ
SHAG
SHUE
SLOB
TAPE
URAL
VARY
WHET

5 Letters

ACRID
AIDAN
AISLE
AMEND
ANISE
ARENA
BULLY
EIGHT
ENTER
FLAKE
FOYER

GATES	RILEY	ENLACE
HEIDI	SHRUG	GREENE
IDLER	STOOL	HEALTH
LATIN		ISRAEL
MACHO	**6 Letters**	OILING
NAIVE	CLIENT	ORANGE
PALIN	DERAIL	THIRST
REESE	ENGAGE	

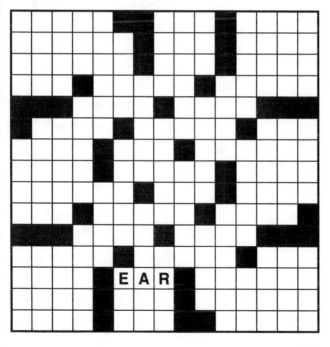

3 Digits

206
207
465
476
595
679
712
752
918
920
972
997

4 Digits

0067
0302
1324
1965
2059
2450
2495
2701
2740
3339
3379
3711
4426
4557
4668
4824
5299
5400
5442
5565
6035
6145
6195
6355
6508
6786
6996
7257
7283
7287
7315
7944
7991
8067
8151
9007
9745
9835

5 Digits

06874
11599
15348
37962
38706
41170
47548
49024
52479
57662
59426
66238
82897

84767	429384	**7 Digits**
89445 ✓	494775	1812775
99706	618251	3251570
	742845	3651686
6 Digits	784662	6158328
247149	927984	6390974
270226		9756925

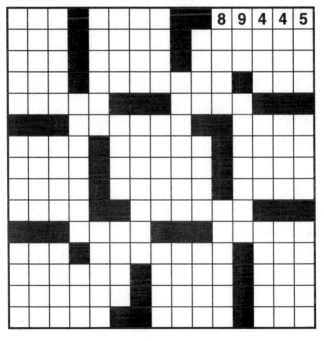

78

3 Letters

BET
BUD
HAS
ITT
LIL ✓
OLE
OPT
RAN
TEA
TIM
TWO
VIA
WET

4 Letters

ALAS
ANEW
ANTI
ARIA
ARTE
ATOP
AVOW
BALM
BAWL
ENVY
ERIE
FEEL
FORK
GNAW
IRAN
ISLE
IVES
KEPT
LAHR
LARA
LEVI
NAME
NEMO
OLAF
OLDS
OMEN
POSE
RENE
SLOP
TIER
TITO
TORI
VASE
WANT
WILL
ZANE

5 Letters

ABYSS
ALOHA
ARIES
ATARI
BASIE
CHIEF
EATER
EVITA
GENIE
HAREM
KATIE
LATCH
LLAMA
MARIS

NAVEL	TEETH	EMERGE
OATER	TEPEE	IODINE
POTTS	TRAIL	LAMARR
PRONG	TROLL	LOSING
SABLE	WAIST	MALIBU
SHARE		MIRAGE
SNIDE	**6 Letters**	OZARKS
STREW	EASIER	

79

3 Letters

ADA
ADD
ADO
BAN
ENA
LEO
MEW ✓
NAH
NAM
OAR
ODD
RIO
VET

4 Letters

ACME
AIDA
ALTO
ALVA
BRAM
CHEW
CITE
DODO
DRAT
ELAM
ELSA
ETON
FRAN
ILKA
IOTA
JOSE
KNOW
LEAR
LESS
LEST
MARS
NECK
NOAH
NOON
OOPS
OPAL
REED
ROBE
ROSA
TOTO
UNTO
WATT
WELT
YEAH

5 Letters

ALIEN
ARNAZ
AVERT
CROAK
DARYL
DRONE
EVERT
HENNA
HINES
JEWEL
NEATO
OVERT
OWENS
PANEL
REVEL
TENSE

6 Letters	SENIOR	LIBRARY
ELAINE	SERIAL	OFFENSE
MADRAS		POSTMAN
MOTIVE	**7 Letters**	STANLEY
MUSLIN	ANALYST	SYNONYM
OCTAVE	ARIZONA	TEAROOM
PROPER	FARAWAY	

3 Letters

COO
END
EON
HAL
HIT
IAN
INA
OAK
OIL
PRO
REA
TEE
VAL
WAS

4 Letters

ACNE
ALEE
ANDY
AUTO
CART
DATA
DEMI
EDEN
ELLA
ELLE
ENID
FOYT
GASH
GIVE
GNAT
HOLD
IDLE ✓
INFO
INTO
LEAD
NATE
OAHU
OHIO
OPEN
OREL
OTTO
OVAL
PILE
RHEA
RILE
SEEM
SHUN
SLAM
STET
TERI
UTAH
WARD
YOGI

5 Letters

ADIEU
ADORE
AKRON
ALLAN
ANNUL
AVAST
BEGAN
COLOR
ELLIE
ELOPE
GLOBE

LOONY	SCENT	ARGYLE
NACHO	STAND	FIASCO
NAOMI	TREAT	GENEVA
NOLAN	TREND	NEEDLE
RADAR	VITAL	OFFEND
READY		REFUTE
ROLLE	**6 Letters**	SCRUFF
SABER	ALBERT	

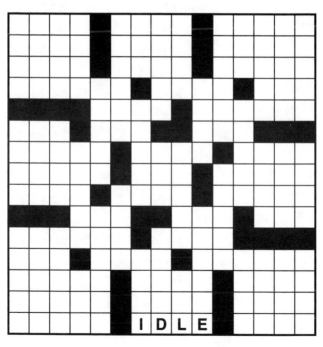

3 Letters

ALI
ANY
COT
ELI
LIE
LYE
PAR
TAX
TOE
USE

4 Letters

ABEL
ABLE ✓
ABUT
AIRS
AREA
AUDI
BERT

DAUB
DUDE
EARN
EARP
FAIR
FAME
GILD
IDOL
ILSA
LILI
LUMP
MAMA
MESS
NANA
NERD
NORA
ODOR
ONTO
ONYX
PEEL
PLUS
RENO
SCAN
SCAT

SLAB
TIME
TREE
TWIN
URAL

5 Letters

ALLEY
AMUSE
BESET
BETTY
BOSOM
DEERE
EDSEL
EVERY
INERT
IRONY
LATIN
LIBEL
NAVAL
OSCAR
RUSSO
SCARE
SNOOT

VINYL	JOANNE	ESCAPEE
WASTE	JUNIOR	RESTORE
	RAVINE	TEMPEST
6 Letters	STAPLE	TENSION
ADVERB		VILLAIN
AUBURN	**7 Letters**	
BECAME	BULLDOG	
CANNOT	ELATION	

3 Letters

AAH
ABE
ERE
GEE
MIA
NEE
ODE
ORR
PEA
RAE
TSK

4 Letters

ACHE
AHEM
AKIN
ALAN
AMES
ANNE
ANTE
AWAY
BONO
CLAY
COMO
DALY ✓
EDAM
ERIK
EURO
EWER
IGOR
IRON
KEEL
KILN
LIES
LIMA
MAME
MERE
MICE
MINI
MORN
ODIN
OMAR
ORAL
OWEN
PLOT
POKY
PULP
REEL
SIDE
SLIM
SNOB
SPOT
TOGA
TONY
WHET

5 Letters

ALIKE
ANISE
ARMOR
ATOLL
CELEB
EPSOM
ERODE
IMAGE
IMPLY
IRENE

KNOCK	RESET	**6 Letters**
KOALA	RICER	DONALD
LOWER	SISSY	ERRAND
MARIE	STYLE	NYLONS
NOHOW	WALDO	OPENER
OCHER	WIRER	SEAMAN
OZONE	YEARN	ZINNIA
PALIN		

83

3 Letters
ACT
APE
ASP
EAR
LOT
MAE
NAY
NIX
OAF
OFT
SIT
SKY
SUN
YON

4 Letters
ABBY
ABED
AFAR
ALGA
ASIA
ASTA
ASTI
ATOP
BEEF
BEEP
BRIM
BURP
CARP
DELL
ELIA
ELLY
ENOS
IRAN
LARA
LONG
LUNG
MODE
NAIL
NERO
OLDS
ORCA
PIPE
REDO
SCOT
SPIT
TALK
TALL
TEEN
TOLL
TRAP
TWIG

5 Letters
ALOOF
ARBOR
BERRA
BRETT
BYRON
DELTA
EAGER
EDICT
FOUND
GRAPH
ILIAD
LEAST
LINDA

5 Letters	6 Letters	7 Letters
NURSE ✓	DOMAIN	ANTONIO
PESCI	EXHALE	APPEASE
SNAIL	LUMBER	ATHLETE
SPLIT	OBTAIN	HABITAT
TONAL	RATION	INSIGHT
	SIGNAL	OPERATE
	THELMA	
	WADERS	

84

3 Letters
ARC
CAP
HAN
LOP
MAC
OLE
POE
PUB
RAW
REN
SHE
SIR
SON
YEN

4 Letters
ALEC
ALMA
ALOE
ALSO
ARGO
ARIA
BEAM
ELAM
ERLE
EVEL
HAIL
HEAD
HERO
IDES
IOWA
KETT
LEIA
LOGO
LOLA
LOPE
LORI
LOSS
NEMO
OPIE
PAGE
RICE
RIGG
SHAW
SLAT
SLOP
STAG
STEM
TARA
THEE
TIER
TORE
TRIM
UPDO
WAGE
ZERO

5 Letters
ALIVE
CORAL
CRANK
ELATE
GAVEL
GRAIL
MELON
PATTI
RELIT ✓

SPEAR	LAREDO	**7 Letters**
STRAW	LIONEL	ESSENCE
UTTER	OILIER	NARRATE
	PLEASE	ORIGAMI
6 Letters	RIVERA	RICOTTA
ENCORE	SEESAW	SYMPTOM
ENTRAP	TRENCH	UTILIZE
ICEMAN		

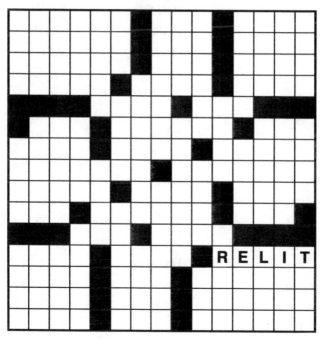

85

3 Letters
ADA
ARE
DON
EEL
EMO
ENA
FOE
FOR
IDA
LAP
MAR
NET
SAP
SAW
STY
YES

4 Letters
ABBE
AFRO

AHAB
ALEE
AMEN
ANTI
ARCH
ARID
AVON
BORE
BRIE
CASS
DANE
DEMO
DERN
DINE
DIVA
DRAT
EDDY
EDEN
ETON
EYRE
HUNT
LEDA
NAPA
NODS

NOME
NOVA
OVAL
PERT
ROLE
RYAN
SCAD
STAR
SYNC
TIDE
WORN
YULE

5 Letters
AARON
ADAMS
AERIE
AMEND
ANNOY
ANTON
AROMA
ARTIE
BEING
CASTS

GATOR	PREEN	GNAWER
HINDI	REESE	LAWYER
INNER	RIVET	MERELY
IOWAN	SWORD	MISHAP
IVORY		SHREWD
LEAFY	**6 Letters**	WIRING
LEASE ✓	AGASSI	
OCTET	ANGELA	

3 Letters
ADE
ALI
ARI
EAT
END
EON
HAD
ONO
SIN
TIE
USE

4 Letters
ABLE
ALIT
ARAB
CARL
CHER
CHOP

DELE
DOSE
EARL
EBAY
EDGE
EDIT
EDNA
FILE
GONG ✓
HALL
HART
IONE
IOTA
ISLE
LAVA
LEAN
LOIN
MELD
NEAR
NEAT
NOON
OBOE
OLGA
OPEN

PLOP
POOH
RHEA
SAIL
SARI
SHOE
SPED
THEN
TONE
TORI
TYNE
YARD

5 Letters
ADORN
AGENT
ALOHA
AMIGO
ASIAN
BETTE
CATTY
EARTH
EERIE
ELIZA

GAZER	REACH	**6 Letters**
GUNNY	RILEY	CAMERA
IDIOM	RODEO	CAPONE
LLAMA	THIEF	CHEESE
MECCA	TIGER	ENRAGE
MINER	TONGS	LOUNGE
NOLTE	VALET	UTMOST
PLEBE		

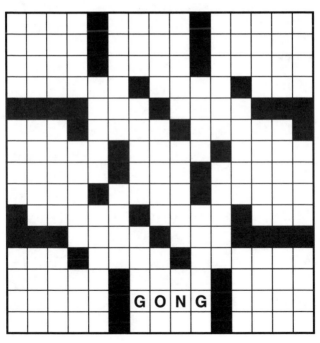

3 Letters
ELF
INN
IRK
ITT
RAY
REB ✓
SAM
SOP
YIN

4 Letters
AIRY
ALAN
ALMS
AREA
ATOM
BAIL
BEEN
CLEO

CREE
ELLA
EPIC
ERST
ETNA
EURO
GERE
HALE
HULA
ILSA
INDY
IVAN
LAND
LEON
LEVI
LIAR
MARC
MIDI
MOVE
OBEY
OSLO
OTIS
OTTO
PAPA

PUTT
RAIL
RAVI
SEAN
SELF
SLAV
SPAN
TANG
TESH
TOOT
UNTO
URAL

5 Letters
ABIDE
AROSE
BEERY
CLAIM
CRAFT
DYLAN
ELENA
EMOTE
EVOKE
FROST

5 Letters		
GIANT	PATTY	BEHOLD
ICING	REMUS	EYELET
LAINE	TAMER	INSIST
LENIN	THUMP	LADDIE
MEANS	UNITE	RECITE
OLLIE		SCORCH
ORATE	**6 Letters**	SLYEST
ORONO	ABSENT	

88

3 Letters
AXE
BUS
DOW
ELI
ELM
ERA
ICE
INA
MAA
OAT
PAT
URI
YEP

4 Letters
ADAM
ALTO
ANEW
ANNA
COLE
CUTE
DOOR
ELIA
EMIR
ENID
ERIN
EXPO
GASH
HEEL
HOLD
HUMP
IRAQ
IRON
ITCH
LACE ✓
LACK
LEND
MORT
NELL
NICE
NOOK
POOR
PSST
PYLE
REDD
RITA
RITE
SURE
TAFT
TEAM
TOFU
TRAP
TUNE

5 Letters
ADEPT
ANTIC
CELEB
COVET
CRUET
EASEL
EATER
ERODE
ETHEL
EXILE
LINDA
LOONY

LYNDA	TOMMY	**6 Letters**
MACON	TRACK	ANSWER
MERIT	TRESS	EQUINE
MESSY	UNION	GENEVA
MIAMI	VENOM	LUMMOX
SLEEP	VINCE	SKATER
SPLAT	WIMPY	SUPPLY
STALL		

89

3 Digits

070
111
260
293
341
349
394
456
570
574
849
883

4 Digits

0017
0259
0405
0477
0629

0695	4273
0719	4810
1009	4852
1012	5137
1254	5249
1322	7304
1639 ✓	7554
2029	7695
2074	7771
2120	8322
2255	8552
2346	8732
2368	9776
2440	
3046	**5 Digits**
3101	00307
3344	05275
3365	20741
3672	21240
3837	21485
4003	22287
4010	27233
4042	31389
4237	33434

34125	78475	**7 Digits**
43647	83344	0032347
43983	84235	0824959
45910	93882	3950298
50484	95525	4031799
69170	98449	7225687
74806		7278143

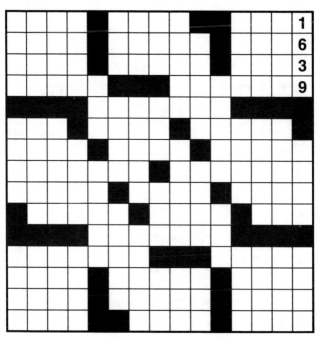

3 Letters
ACE
AHA
EBB ✓
EGO
EVA
EWE
HUE
OHO
OWE
PIE
REA
SAD
SEA
TSK

4 Letters
ACID
ALAS
ALEE

ALGA
AUDI
AVID
BORG
DEAN
DIRK
EDEN
EGAD
FLED
GEER
GENE
GLEE
ILIE
INGE
KIWI
LAHR
LEAP
MADE
MEOW
MINT
MOST
NINA
OLDS
OLEG

OVER
PILL
PONE
RAFT
RAYE
RODE
SMOG
SODA
SPEW
TELL
TONI
WHOA
YEAR

5 Letters
AGAIN
AVAIL
DOLLY
HOMER
KORAN
MEDAL
NANNY
OPRAH
OTHER

PROBE	**6 Letters**	**8 Letters**
RUMBA	DROWSE	CHEERING
SCARF	HERBAL	CONFRONT
SEDAN	MADRAS	GLOSSARY
STARR	NEWMAN	NARRATOR
STROP	PAGODA	STOWAWAY
TRUCE	REPAIR	TENDERER

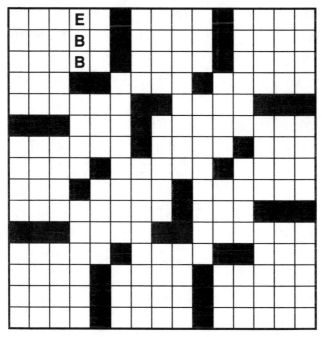

3 Letters
ALE
DIP
EMO
HON
IRE
MID
NOT
OAF ✓
ONO
ORR
PEN
TOO

4 Letters
ACHE
ACRE
ALDO
CHOP
CLEF

DUDE
EAVE
EDAM
EDNA
ENOS
EROS
EVAN
FAME
FOWL
HERO
IDLE
LEDA
LISP
LOOK
ODIE
ODOR
OLGA
PACE
PAST
RENT
RHEA
SCAN
SEEK

SENT
SIGN
TEAK
TENT
TIER
TREE
UNDO
WATT

5 Letters
ACRID
ADAMS
ADMEN
AKRON
ARDOR
DAMON
ELDER
ENEMY
HORNE
IOWAN
KOREA
LAMAS
NILES

OMAHA	**6 Letters**	**7 Letters**
PORCH	EFFORT	AIMLESS
ROAST	MUTANT	DEEPEST
ROSIE	PEANUT	HADDOCK
SCROD	TATTOO	KENNEDY
TEASE	TOPPER	PLYWOOD
TOKYO	WARSAW	REDDISH

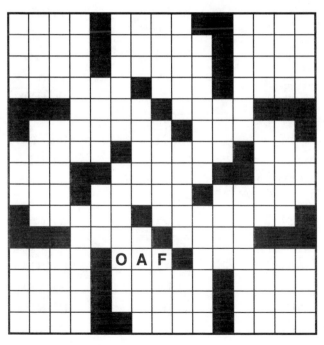

3 Letters

BAT
CEE
DEE
DEL
ERR
IRA
LET
PET
TOW
VAL

4 Letters

ALOE
APEX
ARAB
BEAU
CADE
CAIN
CALS

COCO
DELI
DOER
DRIP
EDIT
ELLA
ELLY
ELSA
EVER
EWER
HEEP
IVAN
JAIL
JOHN
LORE ✓
LOUD
MASS
OPUS
OREL
OTIS
OVAL
RELY
SADA
SCAT

SEAM
SHOD
SLUR
SORE
STAR
TAPE
TAXI
TINA
TIRE
TOAD
URGE
VERA
WHEE

5 Letters

ADULT
ALDER
ALIGN
ARISE
BURRO
CIRCA
ERASE
ERNIE
ESSEX

EXUDE	ORATE	**6 Letters**
HITCH	PAULA	MELVYN
HOVEL	SLOPS	PHOBIA
HUNCH	SONNY	SLEEPY
KEITH	TATER	TEMPER
MAPLE	TIBET	VENICE
MERYL	WELSH	YANKEE
NYLON		

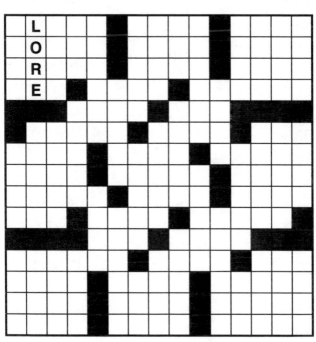

93

3 Letters
ADD
AMI
ARI
ASK
ASP
DYE
EKE
ELK
ERA
ERE
ESS
MAA
MAE
OPE
RUE
TRY

4 Letters
ABUT
ADAM
ALTO
CRAM
ELAM
ERIE
ERLE
IONE
IRAN
NEED
NEMO
NICE
NORA
OBOE
ORAL
RAIL
RAMP
RAZE
ROSS
SEAN
SMUG
SNOB
SUNG
SWIG
TIFF
TRAP
UPON
YALE
YELP
YORE

5 Letters
ALERT
ARENA
CUTER
DEEDS
DRYER
EATER
EBONY
FUDGE
FUROR
IMPLY
INLET
IRENE
KNEEL
LEGIT
MAYOR ✓
NAIVE

NANCY	THEDA	CANYON
NASAL	VOTER	EILEEN
OFTEN		ENGINE
PRIZE	**6 Letters**	LARDER
PURSE	ADRIFT	LAUREN
SARAH	ANIMAL	REMAKE
SCALP	AWAKEN	SCANTY
STEIN	CAMERA	YEARLY

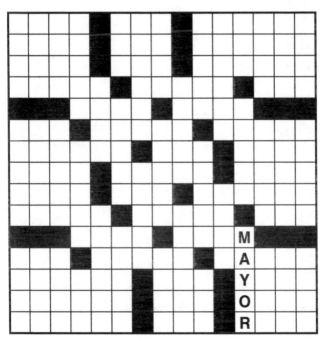

94

3 Letters
ADA
ALI
ELL
ENA
END
HER
HOE
IAN
OPT
SHH
SKI
TEE
TIN ✓
UKE
WEE
WIL

4 Letters
ACME
ALDA
ALMS
ANKA
ANTE
ARES
ASTA
ATOP
CITY
DESI
EASE
EMIR
ETCH
ETON
FEEL
GOYA
HEIR
HOLE
LANE
LEAR
LILO
LUTE
MALL
MAST
MINI
NICK
OPIE
OUST
PERT
RAIN
SEED
SHAM
SLAP
SLEW
SLID
STEP
STIR
TINE

5 Letters
ADEPT
AGENT
AROSE
CEASE
DARLA
ELATE
ELMER
FLASH
HURON

OATER	TWEED	INSERT
PRIME	UNTIE	LESSEN
REMIT		PLASMA
RESIN	**6 Letters**	RECIPE
RIATA	ALCOTT	SALUTE
STRAY	EASTER	SANITY
TONIC	EDITOR	SERIAL
	ENTIRE	SOLEMN

95

3 Letters
AIR
ARE
EAT
EYE
HOG
HUH
INA
LAP
MAR
MIL
ORB
RAP
TEN
TOP
VAT

4 Letters
AMMO
ANNE ✓

ANTI
ARCH
AREA
ARLO
ATOM
BLAB
DRAM
ERIN
ETNA
GWEN
IDEA
IRON
ITCH
LARA
MASK
MAYS
NEAT
OMAR
OWEN
RAFT
RARE
REBA
RIPE
SEAL

SKIM
SLAT
STAT
TEAM
TEEN
TONY
UNIT
WEAN

5 Letters
ABODE
AROMA
ASKER
ASPEN
DRINK
ELFIN
KNEAD
MANNA
NATTY
OPERA
PIANO
RERUN
SHOOK
STRUT

TAMER	ATTILA	**7 Letters**
TATUM	DRAWER	ARSENAL
TRIAL	INMATE	COSTUME
VISTA	NUDNIK	ISOLATE
YEARN	SALAMI	ISRAELI
	SHARON	PASSKEY
6 Letters	SPINET	REBOUND
APACHE		

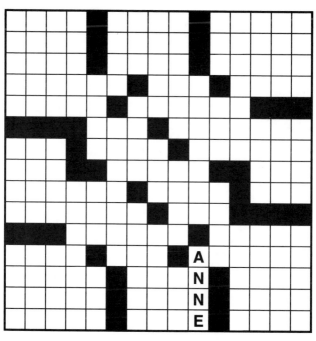

96

3 Letters
ABE
ARM
AVA
GOO
HUE
LAB
LUG
NEE
ONO
REB
RIB
ROE
RUB
TAN
TOE ✓
VEE

4 Letters
AIRS
ASHE
AUNT
BERG
BLEW
BOOM
DADA
EBAY
EGAD
ENOS
EPIC
EURO
EVEL
GARB
IDES
IGOR
INCH
KEEN
LADD
LENA
LENS
LOOT
LURE
NATE
NELL
NIGH
NOTE
OMEN
ONTO
OTTO
PESO
PINE
PURR
RAVI
STYE
THEN
TORI
TOUR
TREE
WISE

5 Letters
EASEL
EBERT
ETHEL
GEESE
HYENA
KNAVE
LIGHT

MARIO	EITHER	**7 Letters**
NAVAL	ELLIOT	ASPIRIN
STREW	ENMESH	BRIDGES
TRADE	LESLIE	DUNAWAY
WHOLE	NUTMEG	ENTITLE
	OBLIGE	SERPENT
6 Letters	PADDLE	WIRETAP
BEHELD		

97

3 Letters

ALF
EAR
HAH
INK
NIP
OAR
ONE
ORR
OUR
OWL
PEA
PLY
RAE
TAD

4 Letters

AIRY
ALEE
ARAB
ASIA
COTE
DEEM
ELKE
ELLY
EWER
FLEE
HASH
ILKA
LEAN
LOOK
NERO
NINA
OGRE
OLEG
OPAL
ORCA
OREL
OVAL
OVER
PAAR
POEM
POLE ✓
POLL
PUNK
RITE
SALT
SELL
SILL
SPEW
STOP
TALK
TRUE
TUNE
UNTO
UTAH
WEAR

5 Letters

AGILE
AORTA
APART
ARTIE
ATLAS
DREAM
ERASE
ERNIE
ESSEX

HOUND	SCAPE	**6 Letters**
LATEX	SENSE	COSELL
PEALE	SNARL	DEEPER
PERKY	SPACE	NYLONS
PILOT	SPILL	PEYTON
REGAL	STANS	SCARED
ROUSE	TRIKE	TELLER
SAMBA		

98

3 Letters

AGE
ALE
AMI
DIN
DYE
EBB
EEL
LAS
NIL
SPA
STY

4 Letters

ALAN
ALLY
AMEN
ANEW
BOLO
CASS
CHET
COED
ECHO
EDGE
ELIA
ELSE
ERIC
EROS
FROM
HEAP
HEAT
IOWA
ISLE
KALE
LENT
LOAD
NILE
OINK
OPUS
PAID
PEKE
PYLE
REAM
REIN
ROLL
SELF
SLAB
SPOT ✓
TIDE
TONI
TWIG
VAIL
WEAK
WELL
WREN
YALE

5 Letters

ABNER
ALOHA
ASIDE
ATOLL
CREAK
DEERE
EARLY
EATER
GRAIN
HEROD

HINGE	ORION	**6 Letters**
JAMIE	PERIL	AERIAL
JERRY	PESCI	ALUMNI
LAPEL	SEWER	CANYON
LEDGE	SNERD	ENERGY
NAIVE	USUAL	GASKET
NICHE	WEBER	REALTY
OCTET		

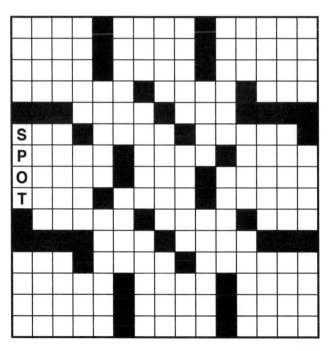

99

3 Letters

BRA
ERA
LAW
OIL
ORK
UNO
VIA
WIL

4 Letters

ABLE
ALDO
ANTE
AUDI
AVOW
CASK
CHAP
DIET
DOUG

EARL
ECRU
FERN
FLUE
FRAN
GLUT
GREG
HALO
HAUL
HERO
HUEY
INTO
IRAN
KERR
KETT
LAHR
LAND
LAVA
LENO
MODE
NANA
OBOE
OLGA
PLEA

PLOT
POUR
RHEA
SLAW
SOUL
STAG
THEM
TRIM
WANT

5 Letters

ACTOR
ADANO
ALLIE
ANGER
BLOND
CHARM
EMBER
EPSOM
FLAGG
GATOR
GAUGE
IVANA
KNELT

LEAPT	ROUTE	BINDER
LEONA	TALON	COGNAC
MUSHY	TASTE	EDWARD
NINTH	TONER	INNING
OATER	TORTE ✓	MEMORY
PESTO		PAPAYA
PRANK	**6 Letters**	URCHIN
REALM	ADROIT	

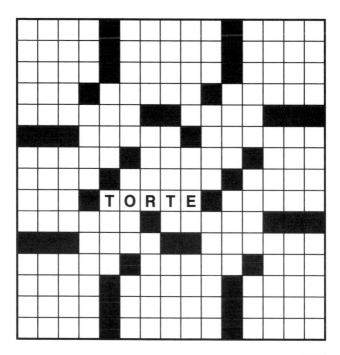

100

3 Digits

271
333
391
478
479
671
728
817
893
930
992

4 Digits

0594 ✓
0833
0874
1085
1096
1193
1226
1359
1547
1841
2178
2236
2528
2706
2757
3473
3562
3678
3997
4152
4359
4374
4758
4843
5293
6434
6632
6637
6681
7611
8014
8649
8741
8769
8922
8950
8982
9144
9690
9793

5 Digits

06441
15682
21326
28477
29209
33222
34431
52228
63452
70699
74457
85736

86190	177016	3317230
97005	308879	3470971
97233	919698	3943956
99990	938986	6912364
		9846389

6 Digits | **7 Digits**
072050 | 0283437
095832 | 2022520

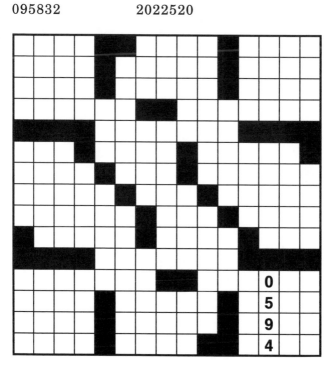

101

3 Letters
ADO
ATE
INN
MAG
NAG
OUT
PAL
PIE
REO
SLY
SOB
SOX
VIM

4 Letters
ADAM
AFAR
AFRO
AGOG

AREA
BAIT
BANG
BEET
BLAH
BORN
CAIN
CROC
EDIT
GOAL
HELP
IDEA
IRIS
IRON
LAID
LEVI
LYNN
MALL
MINX
NEAR
NOTE ✓
ODIN
ONTO
RANG

RANT
RAUL
RAVI
SARI
SOAP
SPIT
TILE
TROT
TYPE
VETS
VILA
YEAR

5 Letters
BABAR
CROON
EERIE
ENOLA
EVENT
GRIND
HENIE
LEROY
METER
NAOMI

NOLAN	**6 Letters**	**7 Letters**
ORATE	BRENDA	CABARET
ORSON	DIONNE	CLOSELY
POINT	INSTEP	GALLEON
RENEW	MIRAGE	HONESTY
RYDER	REWARD	PYRAMID
TRADE	SPARSE	RAYMOND

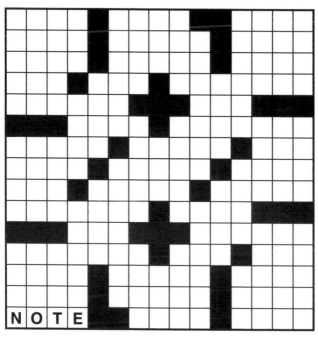

102

3 Letters
CAL
COY
EAT
ELL
GAR
GEE
LON
MEL
OAK
ONO
OPT
SAY
SEE

4 Letters
ALEC
ALEE
ALMA
ALOE

ARES
ARLO ✓
BAEZ
BALI
BARE
BEAT
CIAO
EGAD
ELMO
ELSA
ERLE
EVEN
FEAR
FLAX
HEDY
HULA
LIAR
LOPE
MAIL
NAPA
NEED
NOVA
OATH
ODOR

OPEN
POSH
RUDE
SLAV
STAN
TANG
THEE
UPON
VEAL
YARD
YEAH
YOKO

5 Letters
ALIGN
ANNOY
CLARE
DEBUT
EAGLE
ENACT
GLORY
GUARD
ISAAC
LARRY

LAUGH	**6 Letters**	**7 Letters**
OATES	AGENCY	ASHTRAY
OLLIE	PYTHON	COOKING
PLEAD	RESEAL	DRESSER
STEER	SANEST	NOSTRIL
STROP	TOPEKA	PEEPING
TEACH	ZEALOT	TOOLBOX

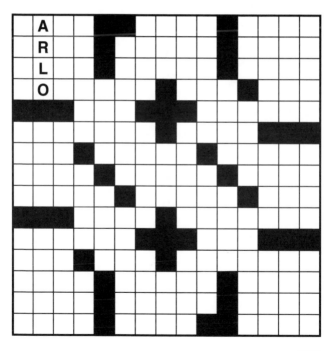

103

3 Letters

ABE
AIR
ANN
EEK
ERE
ERR
EVE
EWE
GAD
INK
IRA
ITS
ONE
ROT
RUE ✓
TAI

4 Letters

ABED

AIDE
AKIN
ALAS
ANKA
ARAB
AURA
BETA
BLAB
BUGS
DERN
DIVE
DOLT
EAVE
EDNA
ELAM
ETTA
GREW
ILKA
ITEM
JADA
LEAN
LENS
MATT
MERE

MONA
MORK
MUTT
ODIE
OMAR
ORAL
OSLO
PITA
RANK
REEK
SEAL
STEM
TREE
URAL
WEST

5 Letters

ALTAR
APART
AWARD
BLANC
DRONE
ELITE
IOWAN

JUMBO	TIARA	INCOME
KEBAB	TIDAL	MEDIAN
LATIN	UNDER	ORDEAL
RADAR		RAIDER
REBUT	**6 Letters**	RATTAN
REESE	AROUND	SKEWER
SANTA	DANGER	SUBLET
TABOO	DIVINE	

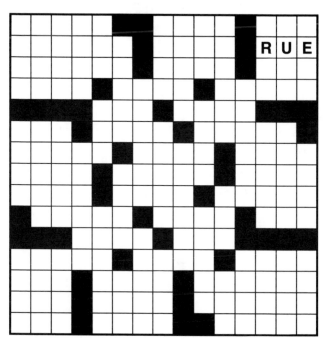

104

3 Letters

ADA
ADD
ADE
AND
BOB
CEL
COO
DEY
ELI
IDA
IRE
MOM
ODE
ORE
STY
WON

4 Letters

AMEN
ARID
DALI
DEMO
EBAY
EDEN
ELIA
ERIN
ETNA
EVEL
EWER
IDOL
IVAN
LEEK
LOAD
MALT
MOVE
NANA
NOSE
OVEN
PHIL
PIKE
PROM
RARE
ROAR
SCAD
SLAW
TEND
VEND
VERB

5 Letters

ABBOT
ADMIT
AGLOW
BABEL
BLADE
DIRTY
DIVAN
DROVE
EDICT
ELECT
ELLEN
ERODE
GLARE
HAVOC
IRENE
LABEL

LAGER	TONGS	LAREDO
LENDL	YODEL	LEDGER
LEWIS		LIONEL
RABID	**6 Letters**	NEWARK
REGIS	ABROAD	OSMOND
SLOPE ✓	AIRMEN	SNORED
SWORE	ANKLET	TELLER
TESTY	DRIVER	WELDER

105

3 Letters

AIL
ALI
AMY
ASP
BAG
BRA
DEL
EEL
ELK
EYE
HAT
HON
INA
ROE
RON
TIA
UMA
WET

4 Letters

ABEL
ACHE
ACME
ANTI
ARIA
ASTI
AUDI
BEEF
BYTE
DEFT
ECHO
ELLE
EMIT
ERIE
ERIK
EXIT
GASH
GENE
GILA
KNEE
LADD
LAUD
LODE

MAYA
MIME
MIRA
OBOE
PESO
SPED
TYNE ✓
WEPT
WHAT

5 Letters

ABNER
ALAMO
ALLEY
AXIOM
DETER
ELATE
ELTON
EMBED
FIERY
HABIT
IDEAL
LAMAS
LATKE

LEONI MEARA MOLDY PINTO RILEY ROBIN SHREW STARR

TIGER UNPIN WALES

6 Letters
AFRAID
ASSAIL
EDITOR

ENLACE FITFUL LAWYER LAYMEN MARINA STOLEN YOGURT

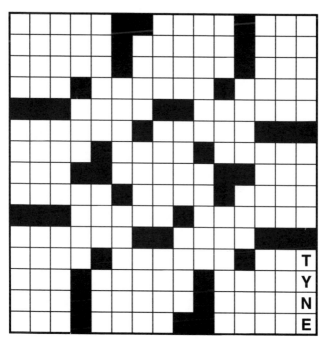

106

3 Letters

AAH
DOW
EMO
HEN
LIL
LYE
MIL
NIA
OLD
PAL
PEA
POL
SIC
SON
TIE
TRY
USE

4 Letters

AHOY
AIRS
ALIT
ANNE
ANTE
ASEA
ASIA
ATOM
AWAY
BLIP
DANE
DYAN
ERIC
ERMA
EVER
FARM
FLAP
HAYS
LEDA
LIFE
LORD
LOWE
LUMP

MARS
MESA
METE
OLAF
OPAL
PASS
PETE
RAVE
RICH
TELL
VAST
YALE
YELL

5 Letters

AFIRE
ARMOR
ATARI
COBRA
DELHI
ERROR
ESSEX
GREET
INLAY

LLOYD
NILES ✓
REPLY
SLEET
TORSO
YEAST

6 Letters
ANYONE
APOLLO
ASHORE
CANYON
DALLAS
EAGLET
ELAPSE

ENDIVE
FLAXEN
PAPAYA
PINATA
SAWYER
SNITCH
STREEP

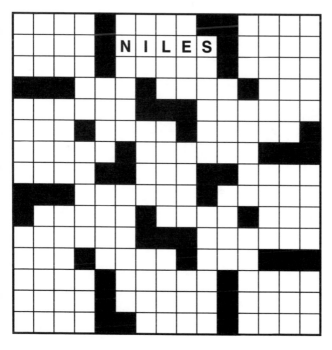

107

3 Letters

AMI
ANT
ANY
ARC
CON
COY
DON
ELM
GOO
LOU ✓
MEW
NAN
NOR
OAF
OHO
OLE
SPA
TEE
TIL

4 Letters

AGOG
ALEC
ALTO
CELL
COMO
EASE
EDIE
ELKE
FLOE
HALF
ITCH
LORI
MESS
MITT
MOSS
NELL
OAHU
OBEY
OGLE
OLEG
OMEN
OWEN
PATH
PLAY

PLOP
REAL
RUST
SEEK
SHOP
SOFA
SOLO
SOON
STIR
THAN
TOLL
TOOK
YOKO
YULE

5 Letters

ABATE
AFOOT
ASSET
AVOID
BOONE
CLERK
EMOTE
EVERT
INLET

KNIFE	ROSIE	ENTOMB
LOGIC	SCRAP	HOSTEL
LOTTO	SNIDE	MARBLE
OCTET	STAGE	PUEBLO
ONSET		SNOOTY
ORONO	**6 Letters**	SYMBOL
PAULA	BAYING	
PIGGY	CASINO	

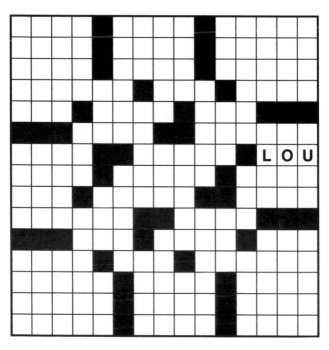

108

3 Letters

ALL ✓
ASK
EGG
ERA
ERE
JOG
LID
MAT
RYE
STU
URN
VIN

4 Letters

AFAR
AKIN
ALDA
ALEE
ALUM
ANKA
AREA
ATOP
BANK
BONE
CARR
CREE
EARL
ECRU
ENOS
FISH
GIGI
GLEN
HOPE
ILKA
IOTA
LENA
LOCO
LOFT
LOGO
LONG
MAKO
MOLD
OMAR

RAVI
REAR
REDO
REEL
ROPE
SCOT
SLED
SUNG
TAOS
TATE
TIER
TRAP
URAL

5 Letters

AGATE
ALTAR
ARENA
CACTI
CANON
CEDAR
CELEB
CLIMB
DANES

DOBIE	RANCH	CASTRO
FLAGG	RAOUL	ERRING
FLESH	REGAL	LOCATE
FORTY	TABLE	NOODLE
GATES	UNITE	NOTARY
GNARL		OYSTER
JULIA	**6 Letters**	RETURN
ORDER	ATTEST	

109

3 Letters
ACT
ADO
AHA
AIR
ARE
ATE
BAN
CUR
ELL
END
HEP
HOE
LEE ✓
LEO
ODE
ONO
PER
RIP
ROD

4 Letters
ACID
AIDE
ALAN
BONO
BORG
CARE
CRAB
DINE
DINO
EDNA
EVEL
EYRE
GWEN
HAIL
HERE
IGOR
NEST
ONTO
RAYE
REBA
REEF
ROOM
TARA

TEEM
TOIL
TREE
VAMP
VETS

5 Letters
AARON
ABOVE
ASHEN
ASNER
AVAIL
CHEEP
CONDO
DANTE
DAVIS
DIANA
EGRET
ELOPE
HEART
HOGAN
INANE
LABOR
LEIGH

MERGE	STACK	COBWEB
NIECE	STEAL	IRONIC
NOBEL	TALON	LUSTER
OLDIE	WRIST	OZARKS
OZONE		TEETHE
PILAF	**6 Letters**	WIENER
PLANE	ASSIGN	
ROBOT	BLEACH	

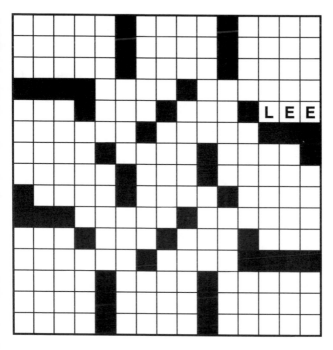

110

3 Digits

000
023
071
090
157
160
203
221
405
419 ✓
500
535
681
729
860

4 Digits

0298
0416

0441
0638
0833
1010
1344
1672
2699
2701
2998
3123
3733
3962
4001
4827
4913
5272
5347
5503
5622
5686
6598
6841
6968
7413

7835
8069
8102
8596
8687
8815
8859
9059
9069
9807

5 Digits

03974
08325
10485
14418
15232
18088
18898
24926
26431
28140
30132
32542

32854	68552	264720
37840	71265	418435
42654	78352	434982
49335	83307	480452
52625	96438	862946
53911		917911
58100	**6 Digits**	974079
63083	142042	

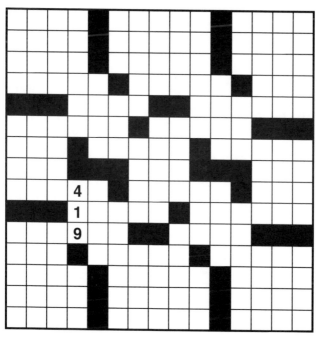

3 Letters

AGE
AND
APT
BEE
EGO
ERR
GAS
GOB
HOT
IAN
IRA
LEA
OIL
OOH
POL
POW
ROO
YEP

4 Letters

ADAM
AMEN
AUNT
AURA
AUTO
BARR
BOLT
DEAR
DEEM
DIRE
DRAT
DREW
EDAM
ERIN
EROS
INCA
INGA
LAOS
LESS
NICE
ODIN
OPIE
OREL

PETE
RAKE
RASP
RENO
ROSA
SANE ✓
STEP
TONI
TORE
UNIT
VINE

5 Letters

ABIDE
AGILE
ALTER
ANGST
ARRAY
CAIRO
CAPER
CROOK
DRILL
ESSEX
HENRY

HESSE	RENEE	EARTHY
IDLER	STENO	IODINE
LINDA	STUDY	LETTER
LINEN	TIARA	ONWARD
LOUIE	TOAST	REVIEW
OPRAH		STITCH
RADIO	**6 Letters**	TRYING
RELAX	BEHOLD	

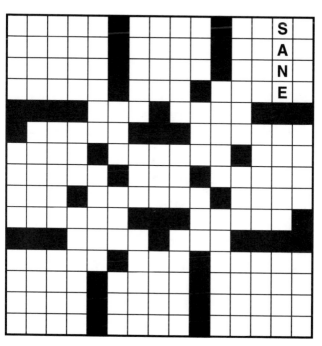

3 Letters

AMI
ANN
ARK
ASP
BRR
EEK
GUY
INA
NAT
NEE
NET
OPE
PAN
PEN
PUN
SIC
SKI
TIA
TIC

UMA

4 Letters

ABLE
ASIA
DISC
DOER
DUET
EASE
ELSA
ELSE
ENID
ETNA
HYMN
IDOL
INFO
IONE
ISLE
LORI
MEAL
MILL
OATH
OBEY
OGLE

OLGA
OMIT
PEEL
PUNT
REAM
RYAN
SEAR
SELL
SHOP
SLAM
SNIT
SOOT
TAKE
TEAR
TENT
TERN
TOOT
UGLY
YOGI

5 Letters

AGREE
AIDAN
ALOFT

BLIMP	ROLLE	ENTITLE
GAFFE	ROOST ✓	ESCAPEE
INLET	ROSIE	GENUINE
KNACK	STIFF	SECTION
LENIN	TEENY	SHUTEYE
LOOSE		UNICORN
MOOLA	**7 Letters**	UPSCALE
REESE	APTNESS	

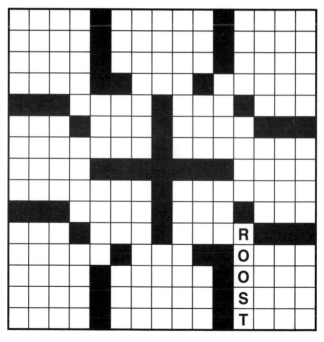

113

3 Letters

ANT
DEY
DOE
ELF
ESS
ICE
LAP
MOE
NIA
REA

4 Letters

AGOG
ALDA
ANEW
ARIA
ASEA
ASHE
ASTA ✓

BALI
BASH
BEAN
CANE
CHAT
DOLL
EASY
ECHO
ELIA
ERLE
ESPY
FAYE
GENT
IDEA
ILSA
IRON
KNEW
LAHR
LIFT
NAIL
NOEL
OVEN
PERM
ROAR

RULE
SEEN
SHEA
SHIN
SIAM
SOON
SPAR
TALC
WEST

5 Letters

ACRID
AHEAD
ALTAR
DROOL
ELDER
ERICA
GNASH
GOOSE
GRASP
HOAGY
INGOT
LATHE
NURSE

OBAMA
PASSE
SARAN
SCONE
SHALT
SHINE
STATE
TALIA

TASTE
UNIFY
VALOR

6 Letters
AIRMAN
ARREST
AWNING

HARDEN
HIATUS
INCITE
MARACA
RACKET
RATING
THENCE

114

3 Letters
ALF
ARE
ATE
AXE
BUN
DEN
EGG
ENA ✓
ERA
HUH
JOB
LIL
LON
NOG
OUR
PRY

4 Letters
AHEM
AIDE
ALEC
DROP
EARP
ECRU
EDGY
EDNA
HAVE
HOAR
ICON
ILKA
INTO
IRAN
LANA
LAVA
LEND
LOCO
MAMA
MOON
MOPE
NEED
NOOK
ORCA
OXEN
PEST
PIED
SIGN
SOME
TEND
TROD
UPON

5 Letters
ALPHA
AMEND
BEGAN
BLADE
CANOE
CLAMP
DEBUT
ELENA
ENTRY
FRYER
IDIOM
INANE
JANET
KLINE
LITER

MELEE

NIVEN

OILER

ORONO

OSCAR

RHINO

SNAIL

6 Letters

ACCRUE

ACTIVE

CRINGE

DYNAMO

KRAMER

LARDER

LIABLE

LIVELY

OLIVER

STILTS

TONING

UPSHOT

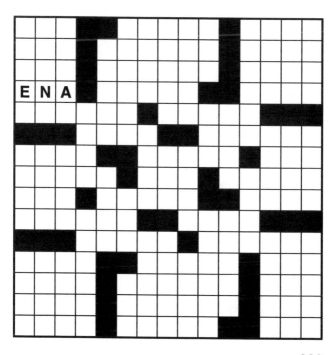

115

3 Letters
ADA
AIL
ARI
DUE
ELK
EVA ✓
IKE
ODD
OLE
ONE
ONO
RAM
RAP
RIO
ROE
STU
TAD
USE
WED

4 Letters
AIDA
ALDO
ALLY
ANTE
ARES
AUDI
CEDE
DEED
DELI
DIOR
DODD
EDEN
EDIE
ELKE
ERIE
ERMA
EVEL
HAIR
HAUL
HEED
HERO
IVAN
LAIR

LEAF
LEER
LEIF
MUSH
NAME
NULL
ODOR
OMEN
ORAL
PAPA
POLO
SACK
SAND
TRIP
UNDO
WARD
YODA

5 Letters
AARON
ADORE
CESAR
DARLA
DECAF

ERODE	SWANK	LAREDO
EVADE	TOWEL	OPENER
HINDU	UNITE	REFUTE
LANKY	WOULD	RENOWN
LORNE		REPEAL
MOPED	**6 Letters**	TAMALE
ORDER	ASYLUM	
SEOUL	DILLON	

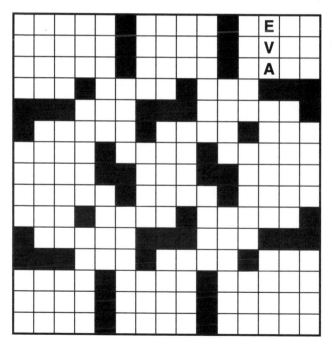

116

3 Letters
AND
AVA
AYE
BAA
CAT
DEE
DUB
EAT
ELL ✓
FAR
HAG
HIT
ILK
MIA
MUD
OPT
TAM
TEE
UNO

WEE

4 Letters
ABEL
ANNE
ATOP
BLAH
BRET
DART
EAST
EGAD
ELAM
EMIR
FARR
GILA
HALT
HIDE
ILIE
INCA
ITEM
JIVE
KNIT
LAKE
LEIA

LILI
LONI
MAYA
MEAT
MINK
NIGH
NINE
PEEN
PIER
RENO
RHEA
RITA
RUIN
SCAT
YOKE

5 Letters
ABATE
ALGER
ALIEN
CARON
EARTH
EERIE
EJECT

FLAGG
HARPO
HINDI
IMAGE
KATIE
LINEN
NORMA
OPERA

RENEE
SMITE
SWEDE

6 Letters
ASTRAY
ATTACH
CHEESE

DEMOTE
ENMESH
FROLIC
INNING
LARIAT
LENGTH
STEELE

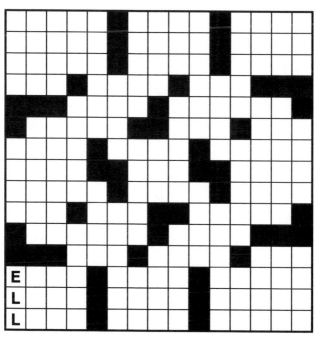

117

3 Letters
AMI
CAN
INA
LIT
NIB
ORE
RUE
SHE
SIR
SIS
VIN

4 Letters
ALAN
ALEE
ALEX
ALMA
ALOE
AMES

AREA ✓
CALF
CAVE
CHOP
CRAG
DADS
DAIS
DARN
DEFY
DIAL
DUMP
EDIT
ETCH
GAIN
GRAB
IDOL
INGE
ISLE
KRIS
LANE
LENA
MERE
MILO
NANA

NEXT
ONLY
PANE
PORT
RAMP
ROLL
SADA
SARI
SETH
URAL
WACO
WHEE

5 Letters
ABIDE
ADANO
ADDER
ADMAN
AGILE
ALIBI
ASKEW
DORIS
HOMER
LYNDA

MIRTH	**6 Letters**	LESSON
NASAL	AMPERE	LUGOSI
NOLAN	APPEAR	ONWARD
OVERT	ASCENT	SHANTY
PRICE	DIGEST	SLEEVE
SALON	ESCAPE	SMOOTH
SHALE	GERALD	

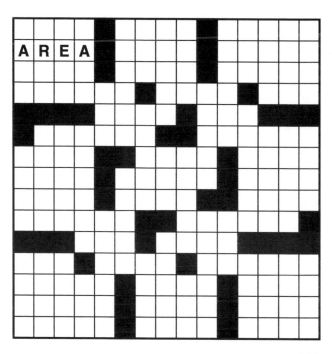

118

3 Letters
AFT
ARF
ART
ASP
BIO
EAR
ELI
LEE
LIP
LIZ
MAR
MOE
NEE
OIL
RAY
TIA

4 Letters
AMID
ASTA
CALL
DENY
ILSA
IRON
KEEN
LOAM
LOOM
MAME
MATT
MINI
NERD
NEWT
NONE
OPIE
OVAL
OVEN
PASS
PEEL
PYLE
RIPE
ROUT
SCOW
SELA
STUN ✓
STYE
TESH
TOFU
WEPT

5 Letters
ABASE
AERIE
AGATE
AGREE
ALIVE
DAUNT
ERASE
FIRST
INEPT
INSET
IVANA
LAGER
MADAM
METER
MOPER
NASTY

RESIN	TREND	MOZART
ROPER	USAGE	MUSEUM
SAUNA		OUSTER
SHAPE	**6 Letters**	OUTLET
SMART	ANKLET	SEPTET
SPURT	ASSUME	SLEETY
STALE	ATTEND	TAILOR
TREAD	ENTAIL	WALLET

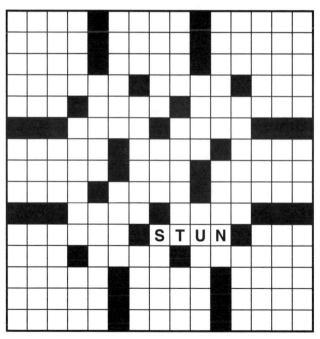

119

3 Letters

AIM
ALE
APT
BEA
DOG
ENA
ERE
GOT
HAW
HIS
HUT
ITS
OOH
ORR
PIA
TIE
TOY

4 Letters

AHEM
ALDA
ALIT
ARMY
ATOM
BOAR
BONO
CORA
COST
EARN
EASY
EATS
ENOS
ERIK
ESPY
ETON
HOPS
LEAN
NATE
ONCE
ONTO
OREL
OTTO

REDO
RENE
SCAN
SPIT
STAR
STET
STOP
TAPE
TART
TEND
TITO
TOGA
YEAH

5 Letters

ACRID
ALAMO
AORTA
BERRA
EMCEE
ERROR
LARGE
MAINE
ORATE

PERKY	UNCLE	MORTAR
PRESS	WHEEL	NEATER
SCALP		OILCAN
SPEND	**6 Letters**	RELENT
STATE	CHANCE	REOPEN
STEER ✓	DYNAMO	SHORTY
TANYA	ENDEAR	TREATY
TEENY	MONACO	TYRANT

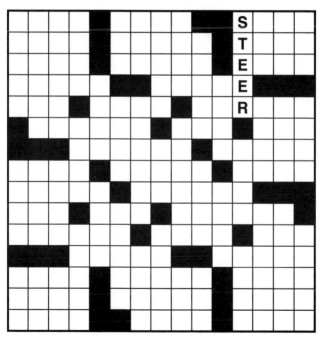

120

3 Letters
ADA
ADE
AIR
ALL
ARI
DEW
DIM
ERR
INK
MAD
MAP ✓
NAN
NEW
OLE
PEW
ROE
SIP
SOD
TOO
URI

4 Letters
ANNA
ANTE
ASTI
CARL
CASS
CAST
ECHO
ETTA
FRAN
LAND
LIAR
PANT
PEAT
PLEA
PONY
PSST
RAFT
SEAN
SEAT
SEER
SKIT
SORE
STEM

STEP
TANG
TIRE
UNIT
WRAP

5 Letters
AARON
ADAIR
ADLAI
ALTAR
APTER
ASKER
ATLAS
CONTE
CREDO
DEERE
HAVEN
IDLER
INANE
KNEAD
MANNA
MARIE
MINEO

MODEL	TENOR	ATTEST
ROAST	TOPIC	HANGAR
SASHA		LITANY
SCRUB	**6 Letters**	PREACH
SHARI	APPALL	RECIPE
STEVE	ARABIC	SNITCH
TASTE	ARCHIE	UNLACE

121

3 Digits

174
181
191
280
299
307
395
398
518
583
594
601
617
645
685
692
737
838
873
996

4 Digits

0255
0386
0792
1093
1428
1617
1989
2090
2417
2503
3293
4307
4833
5149
5221
5516
5579
5682
5942
6027
6419
6837
7981

8210 ✓
8266
8649
8882
9261
9271
9381
9496
9852

5 Digits

10508
33217
35525
36464
56600
57224
58247
58642
62307
62660
75698
75846

80831	104935	820388
93486	285811	898067
	360220	934559
6 Digits	435028	979012
009017	532115	994037
020322	541619	
071279	719383	
098016		

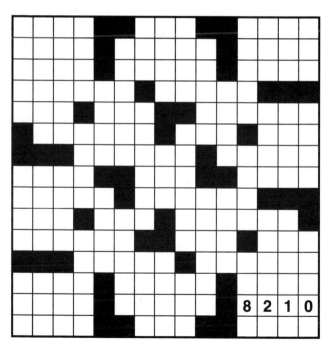

122

3 Letters
ADO
AGO
AWE
EVA
HAS
HAT
HEN
LET
TIL ✓
TOP
WET

4 Letters
ADAM
AGOG
ALEE
ASEA
ASIA
CROW

DANA
EBAY
ECRU
ELIA
EMIR
ERIN
ERST
EXAM
EYRE
GATE
GOWN
GULL
HALO
IOTA
ITEM
JEST
LAWN
MAKO
MAYO
MYTH
NILE
NORA
NOVA
OLEG

OMAR
OSLO
OWEN
PHEW
READ
RYAN
SLAB
SODA
STUD
TEXT
TREY
VISE

5 Letters
ALONG
ASIDE
ELATE
ELLEN
EMILY
ENACT
ENOLA
ETHIC
HUMOR
IDEAL

IMPLY	STRAY	BONSAI
IVORY	SUSHI	ERNEST
KAREN	TABLE	MANTRA
PENCE		OLIVER
SAVOR	**6 Letters**	ORANGE
SHORT	ADJUST	PINATA
STEAD	AIRING	PISTOL
STOWE	ALCOTT	

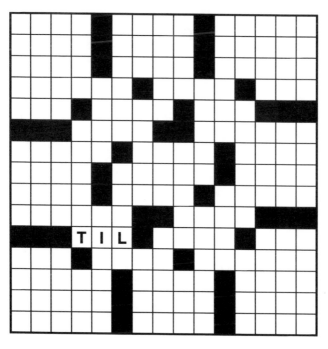

123

3 Letters
AND
BEE
EAT
EBB
INA
IRE
JEN
KEY
LEA
LIZ
MOE
NIL
ODE
PIC
RAD
RED
SEE
SET ✓
SON

STU
TIP
UGH
USE
YEN

4 Letters
ALEC
ANEW
CAVE
CHER
CURB
EDGY
EGAD
ENID
EURO
FLAG
IDLE
IGOR
JIFF
KILO
KINK
LEAP
LEVI

MAID
NEMO
PERU
PUMA
RAZE
RENT
TRAM
TREK
WERE
WOKE
YEAR

5 Letters
AMBER
ASIAN
CABLE
CHOSE
CLEAN
DELHI
GREED
HENIE
HITCH
MEDIA
ODDLY

PRANK	**6 Letters**	HORNET
PROVE	ARRIVE	LAMENT
RHYME	BEDLAM	PHOBIA
SYRUP	CRUISE	TANKER
TEASE	DIAPER	TETHER
TITHE	ENLACE	YARROW
UNDER	FACADE	

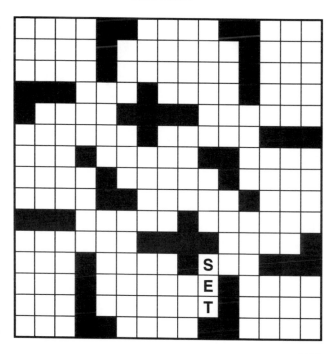

124

3 Letters

ACT
ARE
ASK
BEV
BOD
CAN
CEL
COB
DEN
EGO
END
ESS
HER
IDA
KIM
MAA
ONE
PAT
PRO

RUN
SHE
TAD
TIE ✓
VEE

4 Letters

ALSO
ARIA
ARTE
BABE
BATH
BELL
BEND
CLEO
COLD
DEED
ENVY
EPIC
ERIE
ETON
FATS
FIST
IRAQ

LEDA
LEER
LEND
OBOE
ODIE
OVAL
SADA
SALE
SCAR
SPAM
STAR
SWIG
TARP

5 Letters

AIDAN
ALIEN
ATARI
DEMUR
EMBED
ENTER
HARPO
NIECE
NOTCH

RAMBO	VALVE	IMPORT
RAVEN		KOREAN
ROTOR	**6 Letters**	MILDEW
RUMBA	ALANIS	PREMED
SALVE	ARCADE	SQUEAL
SCOOT	CINEMA	STRUCK
SHARE	DEBATE	SYMBOL
TEPEE	EUROPE	

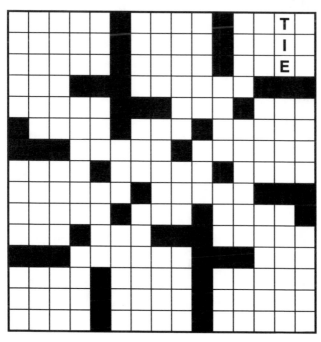

125

3 Letters

ADA
AHA
ELI
ELM
FIN
GEM
ILL
IMP
KEG
PAD
PER
PEW
POE
TAT
TED
TEE
TEN
WOE

4 Letters

AMEN
ANNE
ARES
ATOM
CADE
DEMI
DRAG
ERIK
GAZE
HILT
HOOT
IDEA
ILIE
IONE
JOHN
JOSE
LENT ✓
LIVE
LOOM
LORI
MEAT
NEAR
OMIT

OPEN
OPIE
ROMY
SCAM
SELA
SITE
SLAT
STIR
TAME
TEEN
TONE
TYKE
YOWL

5 Letters

ALOFT
AROMA
BLOOD
CELEB
CRUEL
EAGLE
GAUGE
METRO
MOLDY

NERVE	BOTANY	OREGON
OILER	CAPONE	OYSTER
OPTIC	DRAWER	RELACE
	ENTRAP	STILTS
6 Letters	ESKIMO	WATSON
AIRMEN	NOTICE	WINONA
BANTAM	NOZZLE	ZEALOT

126

3 Letters

AID
AIL
ALL
APT
BAH
CEE ✓
DAB
DAD
EEK
EKE
ERR
GYM
HAW
HUH
MIA
MUD
ORR
PAW
PEA

PRY
PUP
REA
RIO
TAN

4 Letters

ACRE
APEX
DANK
DOER
ELLA
FLAN
FLEA
GNAW
HAVE
IFFY
KHAN
KNEE
KNOT
LEAN
LOOK
LYRE
MARS

MUIR
NANA
NAPA
OAHU
OVEN
SNUB
SPAR
TALL
WARY
YANK
YODA

5 Letters

ADIEU
APORT
DECOY
DEERE
DIARY
ETHER
HEROD
NEEDY
NOMAD
PEROT
PLEAD

READY
STRAP
TARDY
TEXAN
THEIR
THERE
YIELD

6 Letters
BEATTY
CIRCLE
COLLIE
COMMIT
DETECT
EASTER
GEYSER

HEARTY
HORROR
NOUGHT
OCELOT
SOCIAL
STREEP
YEARLY

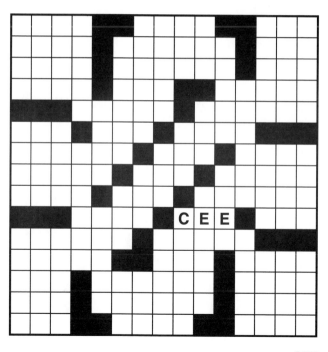

127

3 Letters

ALE
AMI
EEL
ELF
ELL
EMO
ILK
ITS
LAS
LEI ✓
MEW
NAY
ORE
REO
REP
RYE
SEA
SIC
TEA

TIC
TOT
TUX
UTE
YES

4 Letters

ALOE
AURA
BALK
CORA
DUSK
EARL
ELIA
ELSA
ERIC
ERIN
FAWN
GLIB
IRIS
ITCH
LINE
LUAU
MALL

METS
NAIL
RAID
REND
SEER
SPRY
TEND
TONI
TOTE

5 Letters

ALLEN
ALTER
ASTIN
CLARA
DAILY
EMEND
ERASE
ESTEE
INEPT
KENNY
LATHE
MARIA
NOLAN

PORCH
REACH
RENEE
STENO
TANDY
TIMER
UNCLE

UNTIE
WIPER

6 Letters
ADHERE
ADROIT
ASSIST
ECLAIR

GANDHI
INLAND
LEEWAY
LOITER
NORMAL
TILLER
UMPIRE
XANADU

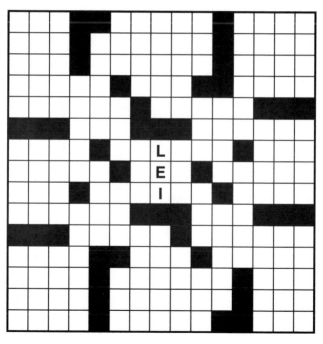

128

3 Letters

ARC
ATE
AVA
AXE
CAD
ELK
ICE
ITT
KEN
MOD
ODE
RAT
RUE
SAY
TOW
YEN ✓

4 Letters

ALAN
DENY
DOFF
EARN
EDEN
ELMO
EMIR
EMIT
EVAN
EWAN
INGE
ISLE
LAIR
LEST
LILT
LOPE
LOSE
MAKO
MORN
MUSE
NINA
OREL
OWEN
OXEN
REAR
RICH
SAFE
SOME
STAY
STYE
TENT
TERI
TEXT
THAI
THAN
TROT
TUNE
WOVE

5 Letters

ADAIR
ADAPT
ADORE
AGONY
ALIAS
CASTS
DAMON
ENTRY

ESSEX   SWEET   FINERY
HAITI   TALIA   GERALD
KNEEL   IGNITE
LEECH   **6 Letters** INHALE
LINER   AERATE   MEADOW
MOVIE   ANIMAL   OUTLET
NOVEL   DEVOUR   PETITE
SUEDE   ELAPSE   SENIOR

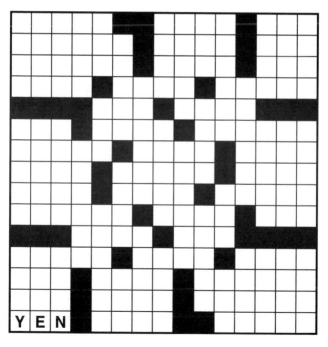

129

3 Letters

ANN
CEL
CHE
DOE
ENA
ERE
ESS
EVA
HAG
HER
LIZ
ODD
OHO
OLE
PRO
PUG
RIP
STU
TAP

4 Letters

ALEC
ARTE
ASHE
BEET
CEDE
CLEM
DEER ✓
ELAM
ERST
HALL
HARP
HOBO
IDLE
LEAR
LUSH
NESS
ODOR
OLEG
REDO
REED
SLUR
SOLE
SPUR

STEM
THEO
TOAD
UTAH
VERB

5 Letters

ANITA
CACHE
COHAN
DELHI
DREAD
EMBED
HANOI
HARSH
OPERA
OWNER
PAYER
RAZOR
SENOR
SNERD
SNIDE
SPOON
TRESS

6 Letters

ALIGHT	HENNER	SATEEN
AMPERE	ITALIC	SERIAL
CHALET	MERINO	SNOOZE
ELAINE	NEATEN	TWITCH
ENCINO	RELISH	ZINNIA
EYELID	RESIDE	
	ROTATE	

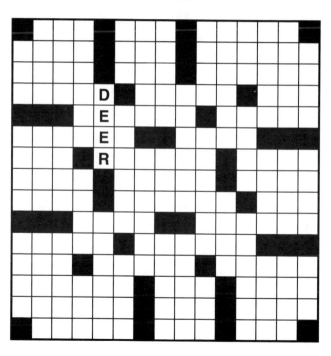

3 Letters

ABE
ADD
AGE
ANY
ASP
BOP
CAB
CRY
EWE
FIT
IDA
IRE
LET
MET
NAT
NET
ONE ✓
OYL
RAM

RAW
RED
TEN
TWO
UMP

4 Letters

ABBE
ABED
ACME
ALEE
AMEN
BALI
BEAN
BEAR
DALI
DAWN
ECHO
EDDY
EPIC
FILM
IDEA
ITEM
LOLA

OBIE
RAYE
READ
REAP
RHEA
RIND
TARA
THEY
YULE

5 Letters

ARDOR
ASTOR
DAUNT
EBONY
EDGAR
EDITH
EGRET
ELENA
FLUTE
FROND
LARVA
LENNY
MAINE

MAYAN
MULCH
NIVEN
ORATE
REIGN
REPEL
TABOO
TEETH

TUMMY

6 Letters

ACCEPT
ATTILA
BARREL
CREDIT
DAYBED

ETHNIC
HANDLE
IRONIC
PARADE
STANCE
STARER
TOTTER

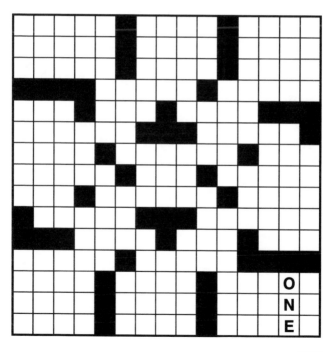

265

3 Letters
ALP
AMP
BAR
DAY
DID
DON
EON
ERA
HEN
INA
LAM
NAN
NIP
OAK
ONO
SOP
SPA
TIE
URI
URN

4 Letters
ADAM
AIRS
ANKA
BELA
CLOD
DADA
DEES
DEMI
EDAM
ETON
EZRA
ILSA
INCA
INFO
KIEV
LAKE
LEAD
LOAM
LONI
MAYA
NEAL
ODIE ✓
ONTO

OTIS
PAAR
RAMP
REEF
RING
SNOB
THEN
TWIG
URAL

5 Letters
ADAGE
ARIES
BURNS
DINAH
ENGEL
GLEAN
ILIAD
INGOT
OZONE
PRESS
SHEBA
SKEET

TRAIL	BISTRO	NELSON
ZEBRA	BLONDE	NOTICE
	CASINO	ROOKIE
6 Letters	DEVOTE	TANGLE
ADVICE	DROVER	VICTOR
AMAZON	ESTATE	WEEVIL
ASIMOV	GROVEL	

132

3 Digits

052
104
137
241
250
261
329
349
352
423
659
708
709
732 ✓
737
751
975
986

4 Digits

0013
0289
0703
0847
1493
1769
1822
2125
2130
2451
2632
2644
3009
3118
3342
3671
3717
3902
4117
4150
6077
6260
6807

7111
7225
7256
7613
7789
8556
9681

5 Digits

00667
01086
02992
05326
06751
08011
18547
20244
21374
23586
29130
40208
45851
52594

53632	89643	470324
57355	90799	473600
58844		560779
71877	**6 Digits**	670257
73148	030618	700931
82828	242782	800430
84626	243110	819306
87722	275044	925179

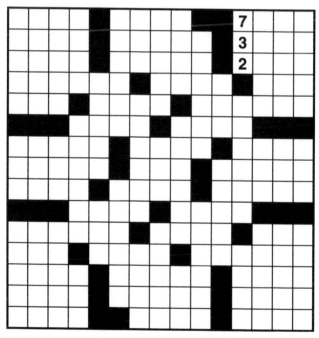

3 Letters

ADE
AHA
APE
ARI
DUE
ICE
ITT
LAS
LEA
LEO
LES
NEE
NIT
NOR
RUE
RUT
SAG
UMA

4 Letters

AGOG
AIDA
ALVA
AREA
CASE
CHAP
CLEO ✓
CLUB
DOOM
EARN
EBAY
EDEN
ERIE
EWER
FATE
GYRO
HOWL
IDES
KARL
LURE
MENU
NEON
OMEN

PAWN
REAM
RELY
SLAV
TERI
TREE
WHEN

5 Letters

AERIE
ALAMO
ALOUD
AORTA
ARLEN
DEERE
EGYPT
ELATE
ELDER
ETHIC
EYDIE
GOING
IDAHO
IRANI

KEANU	SCORE		BONSAI
LADLE	SWEEP		IRVING
LARGE			METEOR
NEATO	**6 Letters**		RATION
OSSIE	ALCOTT		SEPTET
OUTER	ARGYLE		TOLEDO
RERAN	ARTFUL		UNTIDY
RIVET	BANTAM		YARROW

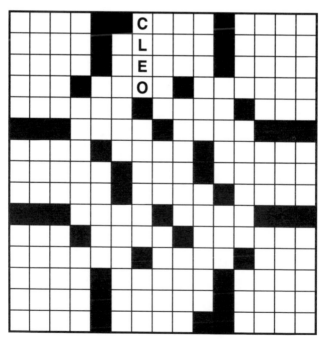

134

3 Letters
AAH
AFT
AMI
ARM
ASH
AVA
CAD
CAR
DEY
EEL
EMO
ERE
FLO
LIV
OPE
ORB
SKY
STU
WAY

ZEE

4 Letters
ACHE
ACRE
ALEC
ALMA
ALMS
ARTE
ASIA
AURA
BAER
BASH
CASS
EMMA ✓
ERIC
ERST
EVER
HERE
IRAQ
LIES
LIRA
LUTE
MALL

MEAL
PERU
RENT
ROSA
SEAL
SHIN
STAT
TALE
TAME
TEAL
TEEN

5 Letters
AGREE
ALIAS
AMONG
CLIMB
DISCO
EMILY
INEPT
LITER
LYNDA
MARIA
OSCAR

PEDAL
ROSIN
ROTOR
SHARE
SLANT

ERASER
HECTOR
INHALE
LESSEN
MANUAL
READER

6 Letters
AERIAL

RECALL
SEQUEL

STANZA
SYSTEM
TRIVET
UNHOOK
VACATE
VENICE
WALRUS

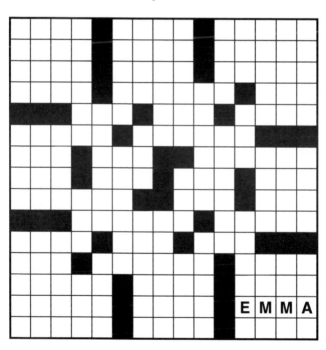

135

3 Letters
AID
BEA
BOD
DRY
EAR
EBB
EEK
GAG
IRE
NUN
OAT
OHO
OIL
POE
REO
SEE
SIT
YAP ✓

4 Letters
ABET
ACME
AMID
AMMO
ARLO
AWAY
BOIL
BUOY
CURE
DRAW
EACH
EASE
ECRU
ELIA
ELLA
ERIK
FEED
FRED
GASP
IDEA
JAVA
JOAN
NAPA

NONE
ODOR
OMAR
OTTO
PALM
PERI
RILE
ROMY
SCAT
SLAW
THEM
TODD
TONI
UTAH
VAIN

5 Letters
ABASE
ABATE
APART
ARMOR
BILGE
EATER
ELIOT

EPOCH	WEENY	ENDEAR
ESTEE		EUREKA
GILDA	**6 Letters**	GROTTO
LOUIE	AGLEAM	KARATE
LUCID	ARDENT	LOTION
ROSIE	ASYLUM	TALCUM
SCOFF	CASTLE	YONDER
SLOSH	EGGNOG	

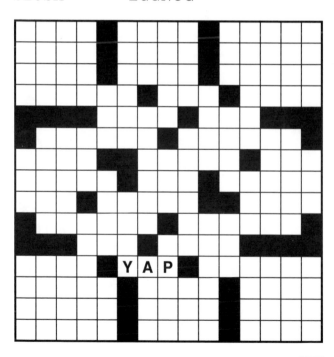

136

3 Letters
AIR
ASP
AWE
BAA
CEE
CUR
DOE
EAT
EKE
ELK
ERA ✓
ILK
IMP
LAP
NAN
PIA
SAM
SEA
SIR
TAD

4 Letters
ANNE
ARIA
ASTI
CALS
DODO
FRET
GWEN
IDLE
KEPT
LACE
LAST
LATE
LEAD
LEST
LIST
LOAN
LOSE
LULU
OGRE
OKRA
OLGA
OWEN
REDO

SCAN
SEAM
SIFT
SNOW
SOLE
TEEM
TENT
TROT
YARD

5 Letters
ABBOT
ADAPT
ASIAN
CREST
DRAWL
EDDIE
ELBOW
ENTER
INLAY
LEACH
LEDGE
NORMA
OUNCE

PAYER	EMERGE	ORIENT
SABLE	ENABLE	ORNATE
SCOOT	ESCORT	REALLY
TABBY	EXPOSE	STOCKY
TITHE	GARGLE	XANADU
	GENIUS	
6 Letters	ISRAEL	
CORRAL	LOITER	

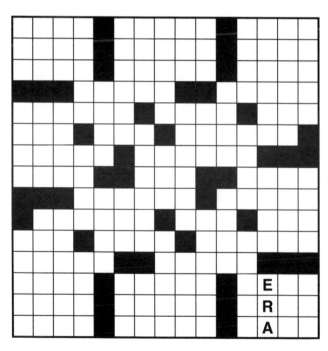

3 Letters
APT
ARC
DEL
DUO
EVE
HOT
IKE
ITS
IVY
NEW
OUR
PAY
PLY
ROE
SET
SPA
SUE
TRY
TSK
YUL

4 Letters
ALDA
ANNA
CORA
CROC
CURD
ELLE
ELMO
ERMA
ETCH
FLOP
GROW
HATH
HOOT
IVES
KELP
LARA
LARD
LEFT
LIAM
LIAR
LISA
MARC
ORCA

ROAD
TALL
TOOT
URAL
VEEP

5 Letters
ADDER ✓
ALICE
ANTON
ATOLL
CHIVE
ELOPE
EMCEE
ENVOY
GETUP
HALVE
HENRY
NICHE
POLAR
SOUSA
SPRAT
STYLE

UNITY

UTTER

6 Letters

COSTAR

DARKER

ESTEEM

HEARTH

HOOVER

LASSER

LEEWAY

LOUISE

ORDEAL

OWLISH

PEYTON

PORTER

RUSSET

STREEP

TWITCH

YELLOW

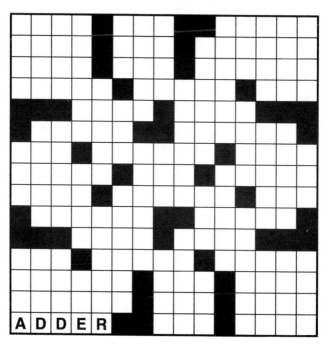

3 Letters
ALI
APE
DEL
DYE
ENA
EON
FIN
INN
JED
NAT
NIA ✓
ODD
OPT
POD
RAT
RAY

4 Letters
AIRY
ALDO
ALGA
AMOS
APEX
ARID
ARLO
BRAN
DEAR
EDIE
EGAD
FLED
GEER
ISLE
IVAN
LONG
LONI
MAXI
MEAD
MEAL
MEAT
NAIL
ODIN
OGLE
OLAF
ONCE
ONTO
OPIE
PANT
PEEN
RAID
SARA
SCAR
STAR
SWUM
TIRE
TYNE
ZANY

5 Letters
ANGST
ASTOR
AZTEC
CRANE
ESTEE
GROAN
IDIOM
ILIAD
JEANS
MANNA
METER
ORONO

5 Letters	6 Letters	
POLAR	AFLAME	ORNATE
ROWAN	EDIBLE	RODMAN
STAFF	ENIGMA	TACOMA
STING	LONDON	URGENT
TWAIN	MARACA	VALISE
TYLER	ORIENT	WILLIS

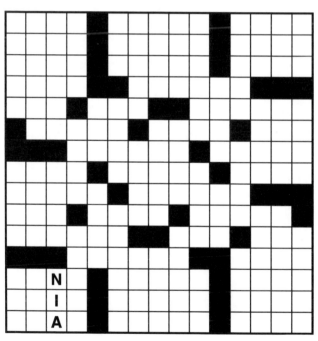

3 Letters

ALE
BAN
FOE
IKE
NAN
NET
NIX
OAF
ORE
PAW
PLY
REB
ROE
RUE
SON
TIC

4 Letters

AKIN
ALOE
ANNE
ARMY
CELT
COST
EARN
ERIK
GOOD
IDES
IGOR
INCA
KILO
LARD
LAVA
LISA
MEET
NEAT
NEXT
NINA
OKRA
OLGA
PAGE
RARE ✓
REEK

RING
RISK
SEND
SLIT
SNAG
SWAP
TAPE
TEAK
TENT
THAN
TYKE
UPON
WEEP

5 Letters

ADORE
ALDER
ANTON
CHILL
CREAM
DRYER
EVADE
KAYAK
ORION

PAPAL	WENDT	ICECAP
PASTE		LOITER
RAISE	**6 Letters**	ORANGE
RANDY	ARCADE	SCRAPE
SMACK	AVENUE	VIENNA
STRAP	CATNIP	VULGAR
TWIST	EAGLET	WADERS
VITAL	ERRING	

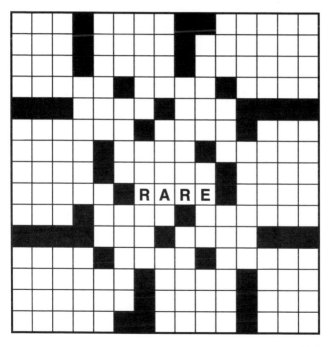

ANSWERS

1

```
A D E   C O R A L   F O A M
L A G   A L A N I S   I S L E
O R R   M E N T A L   E L S A
N I E C E   T E R I   L O O N
E N T E R       N E D
    L A N G U A G E   S H E
I D O L   A U N T   L L O Y D
N A P A   T I D A L   A L D A
C H I R P   S I R E   P O E M
A L E   O B E D I E N T
    V I A       O O M P H
J E D I   T H A I   S P A R E
O D I N   H U R R A H   N I L
A N D Y   E N G A G E   O D E
N A I L   T O N E R   R E N
```

2

```
L I Z A   W H E N   C A K E
A V O W   D I A N A   A S I A
N A N A   A T L A S   L E N S
E N E R G Y   M A S S A G E
    D O T E   E L L
A H A   R I V A L   A L T O
N O B L E M A N   B O R I C
K A L E   E N S U E   G I L A
A R E N A   O N L O O K E R
D R A W   I N D E X   E R R
    R A M   O V E R
G I D D Y A P   A N Y W A Y
O D I E   R O U S T   D O L E
A L O E   O S S I E   E V E L
T E N D   N E E D   R E E L
```

3

```
I F F Y   M E D A L   M E O W
L A R A   E R I C A   A L M A
S T A R   R E A C H   C L A N
A S T R A Y   L O T   H A R D
    O N L Y   R I T E
L A W N   O L D   U T A H
R O N   O I L Y   O R E G O N
E G G   U N K N O W N   A V A
V I E N N A   D I N O   T E N
    C R O C   C A N   V E E R
    T E S H   K E E L
A S T A   T E E   G R A T E R
S L O B   A R R A Y   P E L E
H U R L   T U L I P   S E A L
E R I E   E B E R T   E M M Y
```

4

```
G R O W   B O S S   T A R T
L I R A   I R A N I   O H I O
A L A S   L E N I N   F E A T
D E N T A L   E V A C U A T E
    G E N I E   E N A   D A M
G N U   T O D D L E R
R E T A I N E R   E D G A R
A R A B   N O D   A U R A
M O N E T   V I C I N I T Y
    A R S E N A L   D E E
E M O   R A T   G R I M E
P E R S P I R E   F E E B L E
S A D A   T A M P A   T O O L
O R E L   T I M E R   R O L L
M A R T   T A T E   O K A Y
```

5

L	E	S	T		C	L	A	S	P		S	P	U	R
O	B	O	E		A	E	R	I	E		H	E	R	E
R	A	U	L		R	A	I	S	E		I	N	G	A
E	Y	R	E		E	R	A		K	E	N	N	E	L
			G	W	E	N		H	A	V	E			
P	A	T	R	O	N		L	I	B	E	R	T	Y	
S	T	E	A	K		C	A	N	O	N		R	O	E
S	T	E	M		C	O	N	G	O		P	A	U	L
T	I	N		B	R	U	C	E		G	R	I	T	S
	C	Y	C	L	O	N	E		S	O	O	T	H	E
			R	U	S	T		D	E	B	T			
W	A	D	E	R	S		B	E	N		R	O	M	P
A	N	E	W		B	R	E	T	T		U	R	A	L
K	N	E	E		O	A	T	E	R		D	A	L	I
E	A	R	L		W	E	A	R	Y		E	L	L	E

6

0	7	3	3		2	4	4		2	5	6	4
9	2	2	7		4	1	2	8	4		0	9	5	5
3	8	9	5		7	2	8	7	7		8	9	7	7
6	4	7	0	1	4		9	4	4	5	3	6	5
	0	4	2	9		1	7	4				
8	4	2		4	0	6	7	3		9	3	4	7	3
7	7	5	9	7	9	2	2		7	4	2	3	7	5
9	7	5	9		4	1	3	5	1		8	6	7	5
6	2	5	1	5	5		4	7	3	7	9	5	8	7
8	6	4	7	8		4	2	4	5	0		9	4	2
			1	0	3		0	3	0	9			
6	2	3	3	3	8	7		9	3	0	0	4	3
0	2	0	6		0	0	9	6	2		5	4	1	0
4	7	2	8		4	1	8	4	1		8	8	3	3
1	2	9	1		6	5	4		9	4	2	1

7

I	C	O	N		S	C	R	A	M		S	C	A	D
N	O	V	A		T	H	E	S	E		L	O	B	O
F	O	A	M		O	U	G	H	T		I	D	L	E
O	K	L	A	H	O	M	A		G	E	E	R		
			T	A	P		T	R	A	S	H			
R	I	G	H	T		S	T	I	L	E	T	T	O	
A	R	E		S	T	A	P	L	E		A	W	L	
V	I	E		A	C	E		P	O	P		U	N	O
E	S	S		L	O	V	E	L	Y		P	E	P	
	H	E	A	D	L	I	N	E		T	H	E	R	E
			C	A	D	E	T		A	W	E			
A	L	E	C		I	G	N	O	R	A	N	T		
H	O	A	R		B	A	T	O	N		B	U	O	Y
E	C	R	U		I	G	L	O	O		A	T	O	P
M	O	P	E		N	E	E	D	Y		L	O	N	E

8

H	U	E		B	R	I	E	F		C	O	L	D
E	N	D		R	A	N	D	O	M		O	B	E	Y
A	D	D		E	N	G	I	N	E		N	I	N	A
R	E	I	G	N		R	E	D	O		N	E	O	N
T	R	E	A	D	L	E		W	O	O			
			M	A	I	D	E	N		D	R	I	L	L
P	O	S	E		M	I	L	O		O	S	S	I	E
A	P	E		R	E	E	D	I	E	R		L	O	N
S	A	L	S	A		N	E	S	T		C	E	N	T
S	L	A	C	K		T	R	E	N	C	H			
			R	E	A		M	A	H	A	T	M	A
A	L	M	A		I	D	E	A		O	T	H	E	R
H	E	A	P		R	U	C	K	U	S		I	L	L
A	N	T	E		S	C	H	E	M	E		N	E	E
B	A	E	R		K	O	R	A	N		K	E	N

9

```
E R A S E   C O S T   S W A B
D I S C O   A R E A   T A L E
G L E A N   R E N D   R I T A
Y E A R   A R G O   E T O N
      I O N   A R R O W
  T R E N T O N   O U N C E
S E A R S   R O O S T   O N E
A N D   T E E   P A Y   M A A
P O I   A D L A I   E D I C T
  R O U G E   N E G L E C T
    P E N N Y   A L L
L A M B   A M I D   I T C H
A L E E   I D O L   A L O H A
C O L A   T E R I   P A N E L
K E T T   T R E E   T H E F T
```

10

```
P O R C H   S H A M   H E A D
I D A H O   T A P E   A R L O
A D M E N   A S I A   C L A D
      E S T H E R   K E N O
T O K Y O   C A S S
S I R E   N I L E   C A M E
P L A Y M A T E   A W A R D
E L L   A R S E N A L   R A E
D E L H I   R E S P O N S E
R Y A N   M Y T H   P I E D
      R E N O   E N T E R
K I E V   I N S A N E
N O P E   G R A B   P A C E R
O T I S   H O S E   A D A G E
T A C T   T E S T   L A R G O
```

11

```
P L O Y   A B B E Y   F A I R
I O N E   D R I V E   A C R E
P I T A   M A C A W   S H O D
E N O R M I T Y   T E N D
      L I T   C L O N E
K E N Y A   C L A R E N C E
I R E   D R E D G E   A N N
L O W   E R E   D A D   B E A
O D E   N E A T E N   I M P
  E L E V A T O R   T A N Y A
    R Y D E R   R A T
A J A R   O V E R T A K E
L O R I   C O N A N   E W E R
M A I N   U N T I E   S A R I
S N A G   B O O N E   T Y N E
```

12

```
E L A M   N E A P   S L U R P
L O B E   E R M A   M O R A L
L O U T   E R I N   U S A G E
A T T E N D   D O G S L E D
      A F G H A N
F O R M U L A   C A C H E
R I P E   L E T T E R H E A D
I N E P T   A L E   T I N G E
P A R L I A M E N T   L I E N
  L A Y E R   S T E E L E R
      C A S H E W
B R E A T H E   N E V A D A
R O L L E   S O D A   A B E L
A L I A S   O L E G   S E M I
G L A S S   P E L E   E D I T
```

13

N	A	S	T	Y		F	R	O	G		G	O	L	D
E	L	L	I	E		R	A	T	E		E	D	I	E
I	D	E	A	L		A	N	T	E		N	O	S	E
L	A	D		L	A	N	D	O	N		T	R	A	M
			P	O	R	K	Y		A	P	E			
R	E	N	E	W	A	L			R	E	B	A		
O	X	E	N		B	I	N		S	A	L	A	M	I
O	P	E		F	I	N	I	C	K	Y		S	I	C
F	E	D	O	R	A		B	O	A		D	I	S	K
		L	Y	R	E			S	T	A	R	C	H	Y
			L	E	S		E	M	E	R	Y			
T	O	G	A		E	R	N	E	S	T		R	I	D
A	V	O	N		L	E	S	T		I	N	A	N	E
L	A	R	D		M	A	U	I		S	I	N	G	E
C	L	E	O		A	L	E	C		T	A	T	E	R

14

E	D	G	A	R		S	A	D	A		S	H	I	M
V	E	R	G	E		T	R	I	P		M	U	S	E
E	L	I	O	T		A	I	D	A		E	L	L	E
R	E	P		A	N	N	E		C	H	A	L	E	T
			V	I	E		S	A	H	A	R	A		
	B	E	A	N	I	E		T	E	A		B	O	G
G	R	I	D		G	N	A	T		S	N	A	R	E
E	A	S	E		H	A	B	I	T		A	L	O	E
A	V	E	R	T		B	E	L	A		C	O	N	K
R	E	N		A	W	L		A	H	C	H	O	O	
		H	O	M	I	E	R		O	H	O			
G	R	O	C	E	R		A	S	E	A		A	M	P
L	O	W	E		I	D	L	E		R	A	T	I	O
I	D	E	A		N	U	L	L		G	R	O	S	S
B	E	R	N		G	O	Y	A		E	M	P	T	Y

15

T	A	I	L		M	O	T	H			G	I	S	H
A	N	N	A		I	D	I	O	M		I	N	C	A
S	T	E	T		S	I	N	A	I		A	F	A	R
T	O	R	E		L	E	A	R	N		N	O	T	E
E	N	T	R	E	E			S	U	I	T			
			L	A	R	G	E	S	T		L	A	S	
B	E	W	I	L	D	E	R			T	R	A	I	T
E	T	O	N		B	I	T		A	U	D	I		
S	T	O	N	E		L	A	V	E	N	D	E	R	
T	A	D		G	I	L	L	I	A	N				
			O	G	R	E		S	A	L	I	N	E	
S	C	A	R		I	N	L	E	T		E	D	A	M
T	E	R	I		S	T	O	V	E		E	A	V	E
A	L	T	O		H	I	N	E	S		C	H	A	N
G	L	E	N		L	I	N	T		H	O	L	D	

16

3	4	7	8		0	1	1	4		8	3	3	6	5
2	0	1	6		4	0	7	1		2	9	8	4	8
4	7	6	2		3	2	9	9		1	7	7	2	2
3	2	5	7	9	3	4		1	1	8	1	8	5	0
			0	8	5	9		1	1	4				
	3	0	1	0		4	0	5	8	7		8	9	4
3	0	1	2	9	7		1	6	1	7	9	3	5	3
0	9	7	5		9	6	3	9	2		3	9	4	8
6	0	1	4	8	4	9	3		2	1	5	1	5	0
8	2	2		5	6	0	0	3		7	9	9	2	
			9	4	6		3	1	7	3				
0	7	8	7	2	0	8		4	8	2	7	1	0	0
2	6	4	2	1		0	5	3	2		2	9	9	4
0	3	5	9	7		4	1	8	8		9	5	4	1
5	8	5	4	9		7	9	7	9		4	9	8	8

17

```
M A I N E   U R A L   G E N A
A L V I N   M E M O   A X E L
N E A T O   B L O W   L A V A
Y E N   U P R I S E   A M E N
      E G R E T   R A H
A L C O H O L       B A B A
D E R N   F L U   S E D A T E
A W E   D I A M O N D   C A R
M I S F I T   A D O   T O R I
S T U D       O R G A N I C
      L I L   S M E L T
C L E F   I M P E D E   C E L
R A V I   B O O T   N E R V E
O R E L   E L K E   D R E A D
C A L L   L E E R   A R E N A
```

18

```
K E I R A   C A L S   B O L O
E L R O Y   A B U T   U P O N
E L O P E   N E C E S S A R Y
L A N E   D E T A I L   L E X
      R A E   S N O W
A C T   R E A R   E T H E R
F L I N G   C A L M   E R O S
R A D I O   N I A   M A R L A
O R A L   S E T H   A T O L L
A L E R T   T R O Y   L E E
      S I A M   R O W
E M O   T R E B E K   E A S T
G I B R A L T A R   R I C E R
A R I A   I R I S   A G R E E
D E E P   T O O T   T H E R E
```

19

```
H O C K   B A S E   P A S T A
A V O N   E S P Y   E L L E N
S E M I   W I R E   C L O A K
P R O F   A M Y   H O O P L A
      E U R O   E A S Y
E R A   N E V A D A   G A S
R E P O T   M I S S P E N T
I R A N I   P I T   H E N I E
C A R E L E S S   A R I S E
A N T   A S S A I L   E E L
      P E R T   V O T E
S H R I M P   W A D   L A N G
L O U P E   B A L I   M U I R
A L D E R   I C O N   E T N A
B E E R Y   D O N E   R O A M
```

20

```
L A D Y   H E I R   A S P E N
A S E A   E Y R E   V I O L A
S T A R   R E A M   E X I S T
H I N D U   O N I O N   N E E
      N A P   T R U S S
A M I   D U E T   R E P E A T
P E R S O N N E L   I T C H
T A R A   T E P I D   E T T A
E R I N   R E B E L L I O N
R A T T A N   E R M A   A R K
      A A R O N   A I D
O A T   G R E E R   D A M O N
U N I F Y   P L I E   R U L E
S T O O L   A L A S   C L A W
T I N G E   L E N S   H E F T
```

21

L	A	N	A		W	A	T	T		B	R	E	A	K
A	B	E	L		A	R	E	A		L	A	D	L	E
Y	O	W	L		S	L	A	T		A	N	N	U	L
E	V	E		S	H	O	R	T		S	C	A	M	P
R	E	L	I	C			O	A	T	H				
			R	O	O	F	T	O	P		E	D	G	Y
U	L	T	E	R	I	O	R		P	A	R	O	L	E
R	O	E		C	L	E	A	N	E	R		L	E	A
G	A	N	D	H	I			D	I	A	M	E	T	E	R
E	D	D	Y		E	Y	E	B	R	O	W			
			N	O	R	A				R	E	A	C	T
C	O	H	A	N		N	A	S	T	Y		B	A	H
A	D	A	M	S		K	I	T	E		C	A	R	R
M	O	V	I	E		E	D	I	E		O	S	L	O
E	R	E	C	T		E	A	R	N		T	H	A	W

22

F	L	I	C	K		S	K	Y	E		S	L	A	M
A	I	D	A	N		E	W	A	N		L	A	V	A
N	E	A	T	O		L	A	N	D		O	M	E	N
			E	T	H	A	N		O	N	W	A	R	D
P	A	R	T	Y		Z	E	R	O			S	T	Y
E	L	I		S	E	P	A	R	A	T	E			
L	A	S	S		N	E	A	R		C	A	D	E	
L	I	L	L	I	A	N		A	S	H	T	R	A	Y
N	E	O	N		C	E	N	T		S	A	G	A	
			B	E	W	I	L	D	E	R		I	L	K
S	P	A		P	E	L	E		V	E	R	N	E	
P	E	S	E	T	A		C	R	E	P	E			
R	A	I	D		L	A	T	E		O	F	T	E	N
A	L	D	A		T	R	O	D		R	E	E	V	E
T	E	E	M		H	E	R	O		T	R	E	A	T

23

L	U	M	P	Y		A	C	H	E		P	I	G
I	T	A	L	I	C		F	A	I	R		A	D	A
L	A	T	I	N	O		A	N	N	E		R	E	F
T	H	E	E		A	C	R	I	D		L	E	A	F
			R	A	S	H		N	I	C	E			
P	O	S	I	T	I	V	E		O	V	A	L		
A	L	P		R	E	N	E			N	I	L	E	S
L	E	E		I	R	A	N	I	A	N		I	N	A
F	A	R	C	E			U	N	T	O		B	I	G
		T	A	O	S		R	E	S	T	R	A	I	N
		O	T	T	O			E	R	S	T			
P	O	L	L		A	N	I	T	A		T	H	E	M
A	R	I		A	L	A	N		C	L	A	I	R	E
V	A	N		H	O	L	D		T	A	C	K	L	E
E	L	K		A	N	D	Y		S	H	E	E	T	

24

T	O	T	O		F	L	E	W		S	T	A	I	R
E	P	I	C		L	I	M	A		H	E	N	C	E
M	I	R	E		A	M	I	D		E	L	T	O	N
P	E	E	L		M	O	T	E	L		L	E	N	T
			O	N	E			R	I	O	T			
T	I	T	O		E	A	S	T	W	A	R	D		
L	A	D		D	E	M	O		C	E	L	E	R	Y
I	L	I	E		N	O	R	T	H		E	R	I	E
V	I	O	L	E	T		T	O	I	L		A	V	A
			A	M	E	R	I	C	A	N		A	C	N	E
			P	A	C	E				T	W	O			
S	I	G	H		E	N	D	O	W		M	A	K	O
A	T	L	A	S		S	I	D	E		P	R	E	P
L	E	O	N	A		O	D	I	E		L	I	R	E
E	M	P	T	Y		R	I	N	D		Y	A	R	N

25

```
9 1 4 5   0 9 6   6 4 5 1
9 7 2 4   6 6 4 6 7   7 2 9 4
6 5 1 7   6 4 9 1 1   2 4 2 6
2 3 4 4 9 2   9 1 3 5 1 5 6 6
6 8 0   6 5 4 1 4 1 9
      1 4 3 1   9 4 6 9 5 7
0 7 2 6 7   2 4 6 4   1 6 4 6
6 3 3 1 2   5 4 5   4 0 4 3 8
7 0 0 1   5 6 2 6   3 8 9 0 8
6 9 0 2 8 8   2 0 8 6
      8 7 8 6 9 1 1   4 5 7
1 4 6 7 3 8 7 0   4 9 6 3 9 3
8 8 4 4   4 3 5 9 9   4 7 9 3
2 2 0 5   6 7 5 6 6   9 0 3 6
3 8 4 1   1 9 7   6 9 9 1
```

26

```
B I N G   W H I P     T A R A
A L E E   H U R O N   O R E L
S K I N   O B A M A   L A N E
S A L I N E   P I L L B O X
        E A V E   O L E G
W E S   D E N I M   D A R K
I T T   E R I C     T U N A
C H A I R   D I M   S E R U M
K I L N   N E A L   A T E
  C L I P   A G O N Y   L E S
        T O G S   W A L T
D E L I L A H   T Y R A N T
E L I A   R O M E O   A S E A
P S S T   P R I S M   C H A R
P E T E   E A S Y   K E T T
```

27

```
O C H E R   B E T A   C E L T
G L O R Y   A T O M   O M A R
L O R R E   L O O P   N I N A
E T N A   C E N T   S C R A P
      N I L   H O P E
  A D D R E S S   P A R I S
O H O   A R C A D E   T O T E
R E B   N I A G A R A   W I N
B A I O   C R A V E N   A N D
  D E B R A   N E T T I N G
      S O L E   T I M
E M C E E   A L M A   P A P A
L A I R   B R I E   B A S I S
S L A V   I L S A   O C T E T
A L O E   D Y A N   A T A R I
```

28

```
N A V Y   G N U   C R A M
O H I O   S L U R P   O I L Y
M E N U   H E N I E   S T E T
E M E R S O N   A T T A C H
        H U N G A R Y
  M E R Y L   L U L L   M I L
F I D O   D R A G   E V E R Y
A N W A R   A R E   R A D A R
K E I R A   D I R E   S I T E
E O N   L O I N   N I E C E
        P R O G R A M
G A N D H I   E M P E R O R
A R E A   O R A T E   R A K E
S T A N   N E P A L   L I R A
H E R E   V E G   E L A M
```

29

```
JOHN SIAM THUS
IDEA WILDE RANT
FIRM ELLEN ALDA
FEDERAL DIVER
ORSON ALERT
BLOOM NIGH
OODLES SCALLION
SLOG HOTEL ALVA
SARASOTA LAZIER
TWIG BEERY
BAYOU SENSE
ACORN ANDIRON
STUB IRANI NEMO
TORI TAINT GEER
ERST SPRY EDNA
```

30

```
IDAHO BUST METE
SEDER ARIA ARID
LEONI WARN RILE
ERR GALLEY SEEN
TENNIS NASH
INLAY HAITI
BULB EWE GOLDEN
ONO MELANIE OAF
STREEP RIB ELMO
COINS NASTY
HAAS OREGON
SOFA SHEENA ALE
AVON TOLL VERSE
MARC ROLL EMBED
ELKE OKAY LOONY
```

31

```
SPUN HYPE REPOT
MANE YELL OLIVE
ASIA MAUI OFTEN
STOLEN MOCK ANT
HAN VAT TAI
BOLO LEGEND
SPOOK TEAL EDIE
AUDIE ARI SEINE
KRIS ALAS ASTER
ERNEST LIRE
YON EGG WHO
OWL SPAM NETHER
GREET COMO HIND
RANGE HOAR ANNE
EPSOM ONCE TEAR
```

32

```
JEST APPLE IGOR
ORCA CARON TARA
SOAP CLOUD ETON
ESTELLE OSMOND
EARHART ROY
HAWAII ELSA
OLAF MARVEL BED
SMITH POI LEAVE
TAT OPTING SLEW
ARES EASILY
ABE GARMENT
MELVYN LEEWARD
ILSA CESAR ASEA
SLIM EVITA STIR
SEEP REBEL PINK
```

33

K	I	L	T		M	E	T	S		W	E	E	P
A	R	E	A		A	W	O	K	E		H	A	R	E
R	E	N	D		R	E	L	I	T		I	S	L	E
A	N	D		B	I	R	D		H	I	T	T	E	R
N	E	L	S	O	N		D	I	R	E				
			H	O	A	X		E	C	O	N	O	M	Y
N	I	G	H	T		A	L	L	A	N		P	O	E
A	D	O		K	N	E	E	L		I	R	A		
P	E	A		F	E	A	S	T		T	E	E	T	H
A	S	T	O	U	N	D		E	R	I	N			
			M	E	N	U		E	N	A	B	L	E	
S	T	E	E	L	E		B	R	A	Y		R	A	M
E	A	R	L		D	R	O	O	L		T	I	T	O
L	I	M	E		Y	E	A	S	T		A	B	E	T
F	L	A	T		F	R	A	Y		G	E	R	E	

34

E	L	S	E		A	R	G	O		S	P	O	T
M	O	O	D		S	H	O	R	T		P	O	G	O
I	C	O	N		K	O	R	E	A		O	S	L	O
T	O	N	A	L		D	I	L	L		R	E	E	K
			O	P	A	L		O	P	T			
	P	R	O	B	E		L	I	N	E		H	U	N
S	E	E	M		S	P	A	R		S	C	E	N	E
C	A	N	A	S	T	A		I	S	O	L	A	T	E
A	L	E	R	T		N	E	S	T		A	V	I	D
D	E	W		E	D	G	Y		Y	O	D	E	L	
			A	W	E		E	V	E	N			
Y	A	W	N		G	O	B	I		E	D	D	I	E
O	L	E	G		A	B	A	T	E		R	I	N	D
D	E	L	L		S	O	L	A	R		I	N	G	A
A	X	L	E		E	L	L	E		P	O	E	M

35

F	I	L	M		S	H	A	W		G	R	A	S	S
E	R	I	E		H	I	V	E		R	O	W	A	N
S	A	R	I		E	N	O	S		A	D	A	N	O
S	N	A	R	E		D	I	T	T	Y		S	T	U
			L	A	U	D	E	R		W	H	A	T	
P	A	S	T	E	L			R	I	C	E			
O	C	T	A	V	E		A	L	P	H	A	B	E	T
O	M	A	H	A		I	C	Y		A	S	I	D	E
H	E	R	I	T	A	G	E		D	R	E	D	G	E
			T	E	R	N			E	I	L	E	E	N
J	E	D	I		C	O	R	S	E	T				
E	L	I		S	H	R	E	K		Y	I	E	L	D
S	T	A	T	E		A	L	I	T		O	D	I	E
S	O	N	I	C		N	A	M	E		T	E	L	L
E	N	A	C	T		T	Y	P	E		A	N	T	I

36

R	I	N	K		P	L	O	Y		M	E	L	D
A	R	I	A		G	R	A	Z	E		E	L	I	A
B	A	E	R		R	E	P	O	T		M	A	S	S
I	N	C	A		O	M	E	N		O	O	M	P	H
D	I	E	T		O	I	L	E	R	S				
			E	A	V	E		A	T	T	A	C	K
L	I	V		T	E	R	M		G	R	I	L	L	E
O	V	E	R	T		E	A	T		I	N	G	O	T
N	A	T	U	R	E		C	R	O	C		A	P	T
I	N	S	E	A	M		E	C	H	O				
			C	O	M	B	A	T		F	A	M	E	
T	I	G	H	T		A	L	S	O		F	R	E	T
I	D	L	E		G	R	O	U	P		E	T	C	H
L	E	E	R		A	T	A	R	I		N	I	C	E
L	A	N	E		B	Y	T	E		D	E	A	L

37

1 5 6 7		3 6 4 7		2 9 8 6
9 4 9 9		2 9 3 2 3		5 4 6 0
9 3 8 9		2 2 3 0 7		9 4 1 5
3 2 0		6 8 3 7		9 6 8 9 1
1 5 1 9 8 7		4 0 5 6		
	7 1 0 0		3 2 7 1 5 0 0
0 8 6 0 8		2 6 4 7		9 8 2 8
3 7 3 2		4 0 8 6 9		5 8 2 1
3 0 6 0		0 5 7 2		3 5 6 5 4
6 1 6 2 8 0 8		3 4 4 4		
	2 4 5 1		7 2 4 5 1 3
9 3 2 9 1		7 1 9 9		1 5 8
2 1 4 5		6 3 8 2 3		1 8 8 8
7 6 0 3		9 6 6 7 5		9 8 9 0
6 9 7 4		2 1 8 3		7 4 2 3

38

L	O	N	E		I	D	O	L		A	N	D	E	S
E	T	O	N		N	E	R	O		T	O	R	T	E
S	T	U	D		D	E	L	I	B	E	R	A	T	E
T	O	N	I		E	R	A	S	E		S	W	A	P
		V	I	X	E	N		L	I	E	S			
	L	I	E	N			D	A	I	S		T	A	G
T	O	M		G	R	O	O	M	E	R		R	U	N
A	S	P		R	I	P		E	V	A		I	D	A
L	E	O		O	V	E	R	S	E	E		N	I	T
E	R	R		W	I	N	E			L	O	G	O	
		T	U	N	E		A	S	T	I	R			
C	L	A	N		R	A	L	P	H		I	F	F	Y
R	I	N	G	M	A	S	T	E	R		E	L	L	A
E	M	C	E	E		H	O	L	E		N	E	A	L
E	B	E	R	T		E	R	L	E		T	A	T	E

39

M	E	A	L		B	L	A	N	C		G	R	E	G
E	D	I	E		R	U	L	E	R		L	A	V	A
S	A	D	A		U	N	I	T	E		O	V	E	R
A	M	E	R	I	C	A		S	U	P	E	R	B	
			V	E	R	D	I	C	T					
L	A	S	S	O		A	L	E	E		P	A	T	
E	N	T	E	R		O	D	I	N		F	I	S	H
A	N	A	L	Y	S	T		A	T	H	L	E	T	E
S	I	L	L		C	H	A	D		E	A	T	E	R
E	E	K		A	H	E	M		S	P	A	R	E	
			S	E	R	I	O	U	S					
G	A	N	D	H	I		A	P	E	L	I	K	E	
O	B	O	E		D	R	E	S	S		E	T	N	A
A	L	M	S		E	E	R	I	E		D	E	E	R
L	E	E	K		R	O	A	S	T		A	M	E	N

40

E	A	R	L		B	U	S		M	A	S	K
A	L	O	E		R	E	M	I	T		O	R	C	A
S	A	G	A		A	D	A	N	O		S	T	A	T
E	M	E	R	G	E		A	U	S	T	E	R	E	
L	O	R	N	E		T	I	C	K					
		N	O	S	H		H	I	L	A	R	Y	
C	O	P	P	E	R	H	E	A	D		I	L	I	E
A	X	L	E		C	U	R	I	O		L	I	S	A
V	E	E	R		H	E	A	D	W	A	I	T	E	R
E	N	D	U	R	E		P	A	N	G				
		E	S	P	Y			O	S	C	A	R	
S	E	V	E	N	T	H		I	G	N	I	T	E	
A	R	I	D		R	A	I	T	T		A	V	O	N
N	I	L	E		A	S	C	O	T		R	I	L	E
K	E	E	N		E	Y	E		E	L	L	E

41

```
INGA  REST  CHIRP
NEON  ODOR  RIDER
CAAN  MINI  ATARI
ATTEMPT  LAG  HAM
    TOEHOLD  GONE
FACTOR  RIATA
ACHE    DOMESTIC
IRE  DEFENSE  ROO
RETAILER    CITE
   IDEAL  SEAMAN
FARM  CRYBABY
ROE  ITS  LIBERAL
ORGAN  OPAL  NONE
STAID  MAKO  NOTE
TALLY  EWER  EMIR
```

42

```
MALT  WRAP  SARAN
ASIA  REDO  ELENA
LEAD  OVAL  TEPID
LAMP  NEMO  ROSE
   OLGA    OTTER
PEALE  LOYAL
ALLEGE  BEND  TIM
RAD  YEAST  HOE
EMO  CRAM  ELAINE
   RETAG  ASSET
ABBEY  RASH
BELL  EROS  TYPO
LEASH  COOP  ROAR
ERNIE  HAVE  ARIA
RYDER  OMEN  YELL
```

43

```
GRAMP  CALS  WACO
AERIE  AREA  EXAM
LAMAS  REEL  LENA
AMY  EWAN  TILLER
   ATE  ABIDE
AVOCADO  UNISON
SIAM  VIDEO  NAH
TOTEM  END  MESSY
ALE  OPRAH  LEAP
ARNOLD  APOSTLE
   ORION  ORE
CORNEA  AMID  BIB
LOAF  BEVY  EVADE
EZRA  LEAN  AISLE
FEET  ELLA  LAKER
```

44

```
CRIB  PITA  SHAFT
LORE  ODIN  HELLO
AMOS  MEEK  ANGER
RANT  PARLOR  ADE
ANYONE    ENID
   WEIGHTY  IDOL
OWL  WINE  XANADU
LOOSE  URN  BORIC
DOCILE  OILY  KEY
SLOG  DENTIST
   HAIR  TSETSE
SAP  STAPLE  NOEL
CROOK  SEER  ANNA
ALONE  ELIA  NEST
NOHOW  REAL  TREE
```

45

P	A	P	E	R		S	L	I	M		C	H	A	D
O	L	I	V	E		A	U	T	O		H	E	R	E
R	E	N	E	E		B	L	A	B		U	R	G	E
K	E	G		S	E	O	U	L		T	R	O	O	P
			L	E	S	T		I	C	O	N			
J	A	D	A		C	A	N	C	A	N		A	L	I
E	C	R	U		A	G	E		R	I	B	B	O	N
S	T	A	G		L	E	A	R	N		R	O	D	E
S	O	P	H	I	A		T	I	E		O	V	E	R
E	R	E		S	T	R	O	N	G		T	E	N	T
			C	L	E	O		G	I	S	H			
R	E	V	U	E		M	E	L	E	E		E	L	F
I	G	O	R		L	E	V	I		I	G	L	O	O
T	A	I	L		I	R	A	N		N	Y	L	O	N
E	D	D	Y		L	O	N	G		E	M	E	N	D

46

E	L	E	C	T		T	O	S	S		S	M	O	G
V	O	T	E	R		H	A	L	T		T	I	N	A
E	R	O	D	E		A	F	A	R		A	N	T	I
L	I	N	E	M	A	N		T	U	I	T	I	O	N
			R	O	D		G	E	N	T				
A	B	E		R	A	K	E		G	A	R	B	O	
N	O	R	A		N	A	M	E		L	E	A	P	T
E	A	R	S	H	O	T		V	O	Y	A	G	E	R
W	R	O	T	E		E	V	E	N		P	E	R	I
	D	R	I	L	L		E	R	I	N		L	A	M
			E	A	S	T		O	U	T				
V	E	R	A	N	D	A		E	N	T	R	E	A	T
E	D	E	N		D	R	A	T		M	I	A	M	I
R	I	S	K		E	A	R	N		E	B	S	E	N
B	E	T	A		R	H	E	A		G	E	E	S	E

47

A	T	O	M		S	A	L	T		M	E	L		
L	O	V	E		S	E	R	I	A	L		U	R	I
I	T	E	M		O	L	I	V	I	A		S	I	B
T	O	N	E		U	M	A		T	W	I	C	E	
			N	A	P	A		E	T	H	I	C	A	L
P	A	S	T	R	Y		D	R	I	E	R			
S	H	O	O	K		D	R	U	M		E	D	N	A
S	O	W		S	W	I	P	E			O	O	H	
T	Y	N	E		H	E	F	T		T	E	N	S	E
			A	D	U	L	T		E	S	T	E	E	M
G	E	N	T	E	E	L		W	A	K	E			
A	V	A	S	T		F	O	R		R	A	I	L	
M	I	D		E	F	F	O	R	T		N	U	D	E
U	T	E		R	E	L	I	S	H		A	R	E	S
T	A	R		D	O	L	E		L	A	S	S		

48

G	O	O	S	E		H	A	Y	S		C	A	M	P
A	P	T	E	R		O	P	A	L		O	B	O	E
V	E	T	E	R	I	N	A	R	Y		P	O	U	T
E	N	O	S		C	O	R	N	E	A		U	S	E
			A	L	E	R	T		S	L	A	T	E	R
W	I	G	W	A	M		U	T	A	H				
E	L	L		B	A	K	E	R		N	A	V	A	L
A	S	I	A		N	O	M	A	D		B	A	L	E
R	A	B	B	I		N	O	L	A	N		M	O	E
			B	R	A	G		R	E	A	P	E	R	
D	E	C	E	I	T		A	S	K	E	R			
O	D	E		S	T	A	N	C	E		C	L	I	P
U	G	L	Y		A	F	T	E	R	S	H	A	V	E
S	A	L	E		I	R	O	N		H	I	N	E	S
E	R	O	S		N	O	N	E		Y	E	A	S	T

49

5	1	1	2	8		4	1	8	4		1	3	4	7
2	7	2	5	4		7	6	1	5		0	3	6	6
4	2	9	4	0		2	3	5	6		2	8	2	5
8	7	6		3	6	4	3		8	4	0	3	8	6
4	9	1	1	0	6			4	6	2	3			
		6	6	1	8		3	1	7	2	0	4	9	
7	6	3	0		7	3	5	2	1	9		9	8	2
3	4	1	9	9		6	4	6		0	2	7	0	0
5	8	6		8	2	4	8	5		8	6	9	7	
6	2	0	3	1	0	2		8	9	8	0			
		9	1	4	8		6	4	2	0	2	1		
9	8	0	5	5	5		0	2	3	8		9	7	0
8	7	6	9		8	6	2	6		6	1	4	9	2
0	7	2	0		8	2	3	7		0	6	0	4	6
5	4	3	6		3	0	6	8		8	5	4	8	6

50

F	E	L	L	A		M	A	M	A		C	A	S	H
L	A	Y	E	R		E	W	A	N		A	S	H	E
A	S	N	E	R		R	A	C	Y		G	E	A	R
R	E	D		E	N	V	Y		M	A	N	A	G	E
E	L	A	P	S	E			H	O	N	E			
		I	T	C	H		A	R	G	Y	L	E	S	
S	P	A	N		K	E	R	N	E	L		O	L	E
W	O	N	K	A		A	I	D		E	A	G	L	E
I	O	N		R	E	V	O	L	T		M	O	A	N
T	R	E	A	D	L	E		E	U	R	O			
		P	E	E	N		N	E	S	T	L	E		
B	A	N	A	N	A		S	L	E	W		R	A	M
E	R	I	C		N	A	T	E		A	D	O	B	E
E	T	C	H		O	L	A	F		R	U	L	E	R
P	E	K	E		R	E	N	T		D	O	L	L	Y

51

O	R	R		C	A	A	N		P	E	A	T
M	A	Y		M	A	R	L	O	N		A	C	N	E
E	V	A		A	D	M	I	R	E		T	H	E	E
N	I	N	N	Y			M	I	D	T	O	W	N	
		O	O	Z	E		A	L	E	E				
S	A	S	S		O	V	A	L		B	R	A	Y	
T	R	A	Y		N	E	T		I	N	D	I	A	
E	B	B		D	E	N	T	I	S	T		L	E	X
M	O	L	A	R		I	D	A		M	A	L	L	
	R	E	L	Y		I	C	O	N		A	I	D	E
		M	E	A	N		L	E	V	Y				
M	O	N	A	R	C	H		E	A	T	E	R	
E	R	I	N		H	A	R	A	S	S		H	A	H
S	E	L	A		E	L	I	C	I	T		I	R	E
A	L	E	C		E	D	E	N		S	P	A	

52

O	R	B		W	A	L	E	S		M	O	T	T	O
R	E	A		A	G	I	L	E		A	D	O	R	N
G	A	G		S	A	L	A	D		R	I	L	E	Y
A	D	E		S	I	T	E		I	N	D	E	X	
N	Y	L	O	N	S		I	R	A	N				
		C	A	I	R	O		F	O	R	E	S	T	
L	A	H	T	I		A	N	K	A		E	X	P	O
O	R	I	O	L	E	S		A	R	A	B	I	A	N
W	I	S	P		A	H	O	Y		P	A	T	T	Y
E	A	S	I	E	R		B	E	R	E	T			
		A	L	A	S		E	X	E	M	P	T	
C	H	A	N	T		N	E	L	L		A	S	H	
H	A	N	O	I		G	R	E	A	T		C	H	E
E	L	T	O	N		E	V	I	T	A		H	A	M
F	L	I	N	G		R	E	F	E	R		O	W	E

53

S	I	L	L	S		C	E	D	E		A	R	A	B
A	G	A	I	N		A	V	O	W		F	A	L	L
L	O	T	T	O		V	A	N	E		F	I	F	E
E	R	E		R	E	E	D		R	A	I	S	I	N
			S	K	A	T	E	R		B	R	E	E	D
V	A	S	T	E	S	T		A	H	E	M			
O	C	C	U	L	T		U	R	A	L		R	U	B
I	R	O	N		E	L	M	E	R		P	O	N	E
D	E	W		G	R	I	P		D	E	R	A	I	L
			P	I	N	S		A	T	L	A	N	T	A
D	A	V	I	S		P	A	R	O	D	Y			
W	E	I	G	H	T		P	O	P	E		S	I	R
E	R	L	E		E	C	R	U		R	H	O	D	A
L	I	L	O		M	O	O	N		L	O	D	E	N
L	E	A	N		P	O	N	D		Y	E	A	S	T

54

J	A	N	E	T		G	A	F	F		W	A	I	T
A	B	A	S	H		A	R	L	O		I	L	S	A
U	N	I	T	Y		D	I	O	R		L	O	L	L
N	E	V	E		D	O	C		L	E	E	K		
T	R	E	E	T	O	P		D	E	S	I			
			A	S	I	A		S	T	A	T	U	E	
A	M	P		F	L	A	I	R		E	M	E	N	D
V	I	E		F	O	N	D	E	S	T		A	D	D
I	N	A	N	E		O	A	S	I	S		L	O	Y
D	I	L	U	T	E		N	E	R	O				
			M	A	N	Y		T	E	N	S	I	O	N
O	G	L	E		D	U	B			A	N	T	E	
P	A	I	R		O	K	R	A		G	R	E	T	A
E	M	M	A		R	O	A	M		E	G	R	E	T
N	E	A	L		A	N	D	Y		M	E	T	R	O

55

P	I	E	R		R	O	O	S	T		B	A	S	S
L	O	R	I		A	P	P	L	E		A	L	I	T
E	N	I	D		C	A	T	E	R		H	O	N	E
D	E	C	I	B	E	L		D	R	Y		F	A	R
			N	E	W		A	U	S	T	I	N		
P	R	O	G	R	A	M		H	I	L	T			
A	I	D		T	Y	C	O	O	N		E	T	C	H
S	L	O	S	H		G	A	M		O	P	E	R	A
T	E	R	N		M	E	T	E	O	R		L	E	I
			O	B	I	E			R	U	S	T	L	E	R
C	R	E	W	E	L			T	O	E				
H	E	X		A	D	A		D	Y	N	A	M	I	C
E	M	I	R		E	M	C	E	E		P	A	V	E
S	I	L	O		S	M	A	L	L		O	R	A	L
S	T	E	W		T	O	W	E	L		T	E	N	T

56

D	A	M	E		G	A	B	O	R		V	E	N	D
E	W	A	N		I	R	A	N	I		E	D	I	E
T	A	N	G		D	E	M	O	N		T	I	L	E
E	R	I	E		D	A	B		S	Y	S	T	E	M
R	E	A	L	T	Y		I	D	E	A				
			E	A	R		A	R	M	R	E	S	T	
J	E	T		S	P	O	O	N		O	A	H	U	
E	V	I	C	T		T	A	D		D	E	C	O	R
F	E	T	A		A	R	E	N	A		H	E	N	
F	L	O	R	I	S	T		R	A	D				
			K	I	E	V		T	A	T	T	E	R	
W	A	R	R	E	N		I	N	A		H	A	R	E
E	B	A	Y		B	A	T	E	S		A	L	A	N
A	L	V	A		A	W	A	S	H		N	O	S	E
K	E	E	N		D	E	L	T	A		K	N	E	W

57

S	T	E	V	E		B	O	L	O		F	A	I	R
O	I	L	E	R		O	R	E	L		A	N	N	E
U	N	S	E	R		S	C	A	D		M	I	M	I
P	E	A		O	U	C	H		I	C	E	M	A	N
			A	R	M		A	S	E	A		A	T	E
O	W	E	N		P	E	R	U		I	D	L	E	R
H	O	S	T		I	N	D	I	A	N	A			
O	N	S	H	O	R	E		T	R	E	M	B	L	E
			E	M	E	R	S	O	N		S	E	E	N
D	R	A	M	A		G	E	R	E		E	T	T	A
H	E	M		H	A	Y	S		S	A	L			
A	P	P	E	A	L		S	A	S	H		E	G	G
R	E	E	L		T	A	I	L		E	E	R	I	E
M	A	R	K		E	R	O	S		A	L	I	V	E
A	L	E	E		R	E	N	O		D	I	N	E	R

58

A	D	A	M		K	E	G			G	N	A	T
L	O	L	A		D	E	G	A	S		R	O	L	E
U	R	A	L		E	N	O	L	A		E	R	L	E
M	Y	S	T	I	F	Y		L	A	W	M	E	N	
			T	R	A	C	T	O	R		A	N	Y	
P	E	S	E	T	A		H	O	N	E	Y			
A	P	E	X		U	N	I	T		S	O	N	A	R
S	I	L	T		D	I	C	E	R		D	E	C	O
S	C	A	R	E		N	A	M	E		E	L	M	O
			A	L	O	N	G		F	I	L	L	E	T
O	R	B		L	A	Y	O	V	E	R				
F	O	R	M	A	T		A	R	A	B	I	A	N	
F	L	O	E		E	R	O	D	E		U	N	T	O
E	L	A	M		R	E	N	E	E		S	C	O	T
R	E	D	O		P	E	R			T	A	P	E	

59

P	A	C	T		M	I	C	R	O		A	L	G	A
A	S	I	A		A	C	R	I	D		S	E	A	M
R	I	G	G		M	O	U	S	E		L	I	R	E
I	D	A		D	A	N	C	E		E	A	R	N	
S	E	R	V	E		I	N	A	N	E				
			A	L	P	H	A		Z	I	P	P	E	R
S	E	M	I		O	I	L	C	A	N		E	V	A
U	T	E	N	S	I	L		A	L	A	S	K	A	N
I	N	N		O	N	L	I	N	E		K	E	N	T
T	A	U	G	H	T		L	E	A	F	Y			
			R	O	Y	A	L		R	E	E	S	E	
E	C	R	U		T	E	M	P	O		R	A	N	
R	O	A	D		B	O	G	I	E		G	I	S	T
S	L	U	G		E	L	A	T	E		A	C	H	E
T	A	L	E		E	L	L	E	N		P	A	A	R

60

H	E	D	Y		S	T	R	A	P		R	A	I	N
O	D	I	E		T	I	A	R	A		E	L	L	E
L	A	N	A		R	E	G	I	S		M	E	S	A
E	M	E	R	G	E		E	T	H	I	C	A	L	
			O	A	T			L	I	O	N			
	T	H	I	N	K	E	R		M	A	D	R	A	S
T	W	A	N	G		M	I	S	E	R		O	L	E
O	I	N	K		P	A	L			P	L	I	E	
U	N	O		D	I	T	T	O		S	O	L	A	R
R	E	I	S	E	R		A	P	T	N	E	S	S	
			I	L	K	A		E	R	A				
D	I	S	M	I	S	S		E	G	G	N	O	G	
R	O	A	M		O	P	E	R	A		R	O	B	E
I	N	G	E		M	E	R	I	T		A	R	I	A
P	E	A	R		E	N	E	M	Y		B	A	E	R

61

B	E	N	E	T		S	C	A	R		M	O	L	E
O	Z	O	N	E		T	I	N	A		A	M	I	D
T	R	A	D	E		A	N	T	I		N	E	E	D
H	A	H		T	O	L	D		S	K	I	N	N	Y
			B	E	C	K	Y		I	N	A			
	S	N	O	R	T			O	N	O		F	A	R
A	M	O	S		E	D	E	N		T	A	R	R	Y
L	I	M	O		T	E	E	T	H		R	I	T	A
A	L	A	M	O		A	L	O	E		R	E	I	N
N	E	D		P	A	R			A	B	A	S	E	
			S	A	G		S	T	R	A	Y			
H	O	O	P	L	A		K	E	T	T		P	U	B
A	L	D	A		S	H	I	P		T	H	I	N	E
I	G	O	R		S	A	L	E		L	I	N	D	A
L	A	R	K		I	S	L	E		E	P	S	O	M

62

8	3	6	2		3	8	7	2		9	8	1	7	9
2	8	5	6		3	7	5	4		4	4	5	9	7
1	6	6	2		8	4	8	0		7	3	6	1	7
5	5	8	6		7	0	0		1	3	1	0	5	8
1	3	1	5	4		5	2	8	7	6				
			9	4	6		3	3	7		1	7	6	9
3	8	9		1	2	5	7	4	5	1		5	3	2
5	2	6		1	3	0		7	4	1		3	3	5
9	5	4		8	6	7	5	5	4	2		0	4	7
0	4	3	1		8	8	8		9	7	5			
			0	9	7	4	4		9	8	9	5	2	
0	4	0	7	8	7		9	1	2		4	3	4	2
9	4	1	8	8		8	3	5	9		5	6	7	1
0	0	4	0	0		8	8	0	5		2	6	1	2
7	9	5	7	7		2	3	1	5		0	3	3	6

63

N	A	S	T	Y		S	P	A	N		R	A	V	I
A	S	T	R	O		E	R	L	E		U	P	O	N
S	T	A	I	N		D	I	S	C		M	A	T	S
H	A	R	P		R	E	M	O	T	E		C	E	E
			O	M	A	R			A	S	S	E	R	T
M	I	D	D	A	Y		W	O	R	S	T			
I	R	A		N	E	P	A	L		A	C	N	E	
N	O	L	A	N		E	N	A		O	T	H	E	R
E	N	I	D		R	E	F	E	R		A	M	I	
			A	L	O	U	D		W	E	A	P	O	N
L	A	W	M	A	N		C	E	L	T				
A	L	I		P	R	E	F	E	R		T	A	O	S
M	I	L	K		U	R	A	L		G	A	R	B	O
A	C	M	E		S	I	R	E		A	C	T	O	R
S	E	A	N		H	E	R	B		S	K	E	E	T

64

F	L	A	K	E		M	I	C	E		S	E	L	F
L	O	R	E	N		I	D	O	L		E	D	I	E
I	N	E	R	T		S	A	N	D		M	I	M	E
P	I	A	N	I	S	T		R	E	C	I	T	A	L
			S	T	U		A	R	I					
O	P	T		Y	I	E	L	D		T	E	M	P	
G	L	E	E		T	O	E		A	E	R	I	A	L
R	E	A	M		O	N	I	O	N		M	A	Y	A
E	A	S	I	E	R		G	U	Y		A	M	E	N
	T	E	R	M		T	H	R	O	B		I	R	K
				M	A	A		N	E	W				
A	S	P	H	A	L	T		D	E	C	I	B	E	L
G	A	L	A		O	T	T	O		A	R	E	N	A
O	V	A	L		F	L	E	W		M	E	L	O	N
G	E	N	E		T	E	E	N		E	R	A	S	E

65

```
J U L I A   M O A T   C A S T
A T A R I   I N G E   A S E A
W A T E R   N E R D   N I C K
S H E   M I X   E D U C A T E
      G A R   E Y R E
  C O N N O R S   G L A R E
L U A U   N I C O L E   C U D
I T T   I D A H O   U M A
Z E E   S C E N I C   A T O M
A R R O W   T O A S T E R
      R A K E   L I E
D R A I N E D   B E G   I M P
E A V E   I D L E   N A D E R
A V O N   T I E R   E L E N A
N E W T   H E A T   R E A D Y
```

66

```
B E N D   O S C A R   A R E S
O P I E   W H O L E   F E L T
S I N G   L O V E S   T R U E
S C A R F   R E C U T   A D E
      E R S T   L I O N E L
S T R E A K   O T T E R
A Y E   N I N N Y   C L A W
S N A C K   A S P   L A U R A
H E R O   P E O N Y   L I L
      A S S E T   A N N U A L
B U R L A P   U P D O
A S H   L I N E N   A O R T A
L U I S   R E L I T   D E A L
S A N E   A R M O R   L A I D
A L E E   L O O N Y   E L L A
```

67

```
D O L E   C O S T   T R A C T
O P E N   O D I E   H O N O R
S A D A   N O T E   R A T I O
E L A M   D R A T   E M E N D
      E G O   R H E A
I C E L A N D   A D A M S
N A M   Z E A L O T   L A H R
C R I M E   W A X   S P R E E
H O L E   I N G E S T   C E L
  N Y L O N   N A U G H T Y
      P A A R   I N N
A L L O T   P A W N   A H A B
L E O N I   P O E T   W A N E
D I S C O   L U L L   E L K E
O F T E N   E L L Y   R O A N
```

68

```
D E M U R   D O F F   C L A M
O R O N O   E L I A   L I K E
T I T H E   S Y N C   A L I T
E C H O   V I M   I O D I N E
      O P E   P E A R
  W A K E N   I L L E G A L
T A B   L U C C I   I L I E
A D A P T E R   T A I L I N G
M E S A   E B E R T   V E G
R E M O D E L   O C H E R
      Y O K O   S H Y
B A C A L L   O L E   M A S H
O R A L   L O P E   A N I T A
A M M O   O W E N   R A D A R
T Y P E   P E R T   F L A R E
```

69

```
A C R E   B A B E L   A R A B
R O O M   A D O R E   G I L A
G R A B   T A L O N   E N I D
O D D L Y   P A S T A   G A G
      E A S T     I M P O S E
A L U M N A   I G L O O
S O N   K I T T Y   S T A N S
H I D   L E A R N   G O O
E N O L A   A L O O F   O A R
      E N E M Y   S O U G H T
A T T E N D   B E R N
R U E   A I S L E   E B S E N
E T N A   T O O T H   O O Z E
N O S H   O R A T E   L A R A
A R E A   R E F E R   T R A P
```

70

```
F I E L D   R A S H   E R O S
A D D E R   E B A Y   R I T E
L E A S E   T E M P   I O T A
L A M   D E A L   H E C T O R
      G A G   S E L A
S T E E R   J A N E   O W E
S H I M   N E O N   N O L A N
C O M I C   N I T   A M I G O
A N I T A   G N A W   I V E S
R E D   B E E T   O T T E R
      S I L L   W O W
B I K I N I   S A L E   S E W
A V O N   C I T Y   L E O N A
L A N G   I R O N   V A L I D
I N G E   T A P E   E R O D E
```

71

```
T A C K   G R A B   S A S H
E L L E   E A S E L   E R I E
N O U N   O U T D O   L I R A
S U N   A R L O   W E L D E R
E D G I N G   R E E V E
      O T I S   C L A R I F Y
B O N N   A T O L L   S L A V
E G O   A H A   I C E
A L D A   B R O I L   V E T S
R E S T O R E   R E B A
      L A U R A   A R T I S T
M O Z A R T   B U R R   V E E
E V A N   A D O R N   S O D A
S E N T   L E D G E   A R E S
A R E A   B E E R   L Y R E
```

72

```
G R A Z E   C H A P   L E D
R E L E N T   H A I L   I R E
I N V A D E   E R M A   B R R
M E A L   S T E T   C A R O B
      O C T E T   H I L A R Y
A N N U L   X A N A D U
M O O S E   T H A I   M E R E
I M P   F L U   T R Y   D E W
D E E R   A R I A   A B I D E
      A C C E S S   R O T O R
S P A C E Y   R H I N O
H A R E M   P A A R   K R I S
A G O   E L L E   O W L I S H
R A M   N E A L   N E E D L E
I N A   T O N I     S T E E D
```

73

E	V	A	N		D	A	D	S		R	A	R	E
R	O	S	E		I	D	I	O	M		E	L	I	A
S	T	E	W		N	A	O	M	I		S	L	O	T
T	E	A	S	E		R	E	A	C	T			
		M	O	V	E			M	A	Y	H	E	M
	P	L	A	N	E	R		A	I	R	L	I	N	E
S	O	O	N		E	N	O	S		P	E	A	R	L
H	O	N		R	E	L	I	T			T	I	E
A	D	D	E	R		S	E	M	I		L	U	C	E
F	L	O	R	I	S	T		O	N	R	U	S	H
T	E	N	A	N	T		V	A	I	L			
		S	K	U	L	L			B	L	A	I	R
L	U	A	U		N	E	I	G	H		A	L	D	O
E	M	I	R		G	E	N	I	E		B	O	O	M
G	A	L	E			K	E	L	P		Y	E	L	P

74

A	M	M	O		T	H	I	N		P	O	N	G
S	O	U	P		S	H	O	R	E		E	D	I	E
T	O	R	E		T	I	B	E	T		R	I	C	E
I	R	A		B	I	S	O	N		D	I	N	E	R
R	E	L	I	E	F			E	W	E			
		C	A	F	E			E	L	A	P	S	E
D	R	A	I	N		R	A	S	P		L	A	I	D
E	Y	R	E		P	I	V	O	T		W	I	N	G
C	A	L	S		S	C	A	R		S	A	R	G	E
K	N	O	T	T	S			E	M	M	Y		
		U	T	E			A	U	S	T	I	N
I	N	D	E	X		S	P	R	I	G		W	R	Y
N	E	A	T		A	S	I	A	N		D	I	A	L
G	O	W	N		H	E	N	I	E		A	L	T	O
A	N	N	A		A	X	E	L		G	L	E	N

75

O	C	C	U	R		G	I	S	H		E	A	R	P
S	H	A	M	E		A	L	E	E		S	L	U	R
C	O	R	P	S		L	I	A	M		K	I	L	O
A	R	E		O	I	L	E	R		I	T	E	M
R	E	W	A	R	D			S	W	A	M		
		S	T	A	N	K		I	R	O	N	I	C
Z	I	T	I		E	N	O	L	A		O	N	O
O	C	E	A	N		E	E	K		B	U	T	T	E
N	O	R		U	N	D	E	R		P	E	O	N
E	N	I	G	M	A		L	A	S	S	O		
		A	B	B	Y		H	A	N	S	E	L
S	C	A	N		U	P	S	E	T		P	E	A
T	O	L	D		A	K	I	N		E	B	E	R	T
U	R	G	E		S	O	L	O		E	R	N	I	E
D	E	A	R		K	N	E	W		N	A	D	E	R

76

F	L	A	K	E		A	C	E		S	L	O	B
O	I	L	I	N	G		I	L	L		T	A	P	E
O	R	A	N	G	E		R	I	M		O	D	I	E
T	E	N		A	N	I	S	E		F	O	Y	E	R
		E	G	A	D		N	A	I	L			
	M	A	N	E		L	A	T	I	N		P	A	C
F	A	C	T		G	E	M		D	E	R	A	I	L
A	C	R	E		A	R	E	N	A		I	L	S	A
T	H	I	R	S	T		N	A	N		L	I	L	Y
S	O	D		H	E	I	D	I		G	E	N	E
		B	A	S	S		V	A	R	Y			
S	H	R	U	G		R	E	E	S	E		F	E	W
H	E	E	L		E	A	R		H	E	A	L	T	H
U	R	A	L		L	E	I		E	N	L	A	C	E
E	D	D	Y		I	L	K		E	I	G	H	T

77

```
595   4668   8945
997   2701  742845
476   9835  270226
206  3651686   465
66238      3379
   247149     7257
1965  38706   5442
3711  11599   6508
2495  52479   9007
4557  784662
    0067    15348
752  6158328   712
927984  0302   918
494775  6355   679
49024    7991   207
```

78

```
KEPT  LATCH  OLAF
AVOW  ALOHA  ZANE
TITO  MARIS  ARTE
ITT   BASIE  TRAIL
EASIER    FORK
     STREW  LOSING
BAWL  NAVEL  RAN
ARIES  VIA  LLAMA
LIL   ABYSS  ANEW
MALIBU    TEETH
     OLDS   MIRAGE
SNIDE  HAREM  TEA
LEVI  OATER  WANT
OMEN  PRONG  ERIE
POSE  TEPEE  TIER
```

79

```
 JOSE  ACME  ALVA
REVEL  DRAT  REED
OWENS  DODO  IOTA
SERIAL   ARNAZ
ALTO  ILKA  NOAH
  ROBE   STANLEY
ODD  FRAN  ELAINE
OAR  FARAWAY  ENA
PROPER  MARS  NAH
SYNONYM   TOTO
 LESS  UNTO  CHEW
   TENSE  MOTIVE
BRAM  ELAM  PANEL
AIDA  CITE  AVERT
NOON  KNOW  LEST
```

80

```
OREL  GIVE  AVAST
PILE  ENID  RADAR
ELLA  NATE  GLOBE
NEEDLE  ANDY  REA
   OVAL   ALBERT
WAS  OAK   TEE
ALLAN  RHEA  GASH
READY  OIL  NACHO
DEMI  INTO  ANNUL
   EON  PRO  END
SCRUFF    SEEM
COO  FOYT  FIASCO
ELLIE  OAHU  UTAH
NOLAN  GNAT  TERI
TREND  IDLE  OTTO
```

81

```
F A I R   S C A T   B E S E T
A B L E   N A N A   O S C A R
M E S S   O N Y X   S C A R E
E L A T I O N     J O A N N E
      O N T O   L U M P
D E E R E   T W I N   E L I
A D V E R B   A L I   E A R P
U S E   T E N S I O N   T O E
B E R T   C O T   R A V I N E
  L Y E   A R E A   V I N Y L
      M A M A   U R A L
S T A P L E     B U L L D O G
L I B E L   P L U S   A U D I
A M U S E   A I R S   I D O L
B E T T Y   R E N O   N E R D
```

82

```
I M A G E   M O R N   C O M O
R I C E R   A W A Y   E D A M
O C H E R   R E E L   L I M A
N E E   A K I N   O P E N E R
      A N N E   S N O B
W A L D O   T S K   P E A
M I N I   C L A Y   Y E A R N
E R I K   K O A L A   P L O T
R E S E T   W H E T   S I D E
E R E   O D E   O Z O N E
      I G O R   S L I M
S E A M A N   K I L N   A B E
P U L P   A M E S   N O H O W
O R A L   L I E S   I R E N E
T O N Y   D A L Y   A R M O R
```

83

```
A B E D   A B B Y   I L I A D
R E D O   N E R O   N U R S E
B R I M   T E E N   S N A I L
O R C A   O F T   S I G N A L
R A T I O N   T W I G
      N A I L   A T H L E T E
A C T   F O U N D   T O N A L
L A R A   M A E   T O L L
G R A P H   B Y R O N   S K Y
A P P E A S E   S P I T
      B U R P   E X H A L E
O B T A I N   E A R   E L I A
L E A S T   A S T A   L O N G
D E L T A   S C O T   M O D E
S P L I T   P I P E   A F A R
```

84

```
T R E N C H   S H E   S H A W
R I V E R A   Y E N   T A R A
I C E M A N   M A C   R I G G
M E L O N   U P D O   A L O E
      K E T T   R A W
C A P   L I O N E L   P U B
L O L A   A L M A   E L A T E
O R I G A M I   R I C O T T A
G A V E L   Z E R O   S T E M
O L E   S E E S A W   S I R
      S O N   S T A G
S L O P   T H E E   R E L I T
L O P E   R E N   L A R E D O
A R I A   A R C   O I L I E R
T I E R   P O E   P L E A S E
```

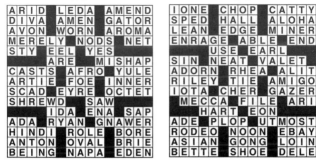

85

```
A R I D   L E D A   A M E N D
D I V A   A M E N   G A T O R
A V O N   W O R N   A R O M A
M E R E L Y   N O D S   N E T
S T Y   E E L   Y E S
      A R E   M I S H A P
C A S T S   A F R O   Y U L E
A R T I E   F O E   I N N E R
S C A D   E Y R E   O C T E T
S H R E W D   S A W
      I D A   E N A   S A P
A D A   R Y A N   G N A W E R
H I N D I   R O L E   B O R E
A N T O N   O V A L   B R I E
B E I N G   N A P A   E D E N
```

86

```
I O N E   C H O P   C A T T Y
S P E D   H A L L   A L O H A
L E A N   E D G E   M I N E R
E N R A G E   A B L E   E N D
      U S E   E A R L
S I N   N E A T   V A L E T
A D O R N   R H E A   A L I T
R I L E Y   T I E   A M I G O
I O T A   C H E R   G A Z E R
M E C C A   F I L E   A R I
      H A R T   E O N
A D E   P L O P   U T M O S T
R O D E O   N O O N   E B A Y
A S I A N   G O N G   L O I N
B E T T E   S H O E   D E L E
```

87

```
O B E Y   R E M U S   E R S T
L E V I   E L E N A   P A P A
L E O N   C L A I M   I V A N
I R K   G I A N T   I C I N G
E Y E L E T   S E A N
      A R E A   I N S I S T
A B I D E   L I A R   C L E O
L A N D   P A T T Y   O S L O
M I D I   U N T O   C R A F T
S L Y E S T   M A R C
      O T T O   B E H O L D
T H U M P   A R O S E   R A Y
E U R O   E M O T E   R A I L
S L A V   L E N I N   E T N A
H A L E   F R O S T   B E E N
```

88

```
R I T A   G A S H   L I N D A
I R O N   E X P O   U N I O N
T A F T   N E L L   M A C O N
E Q U I N E   A D A M   E R A
      C O V E T   D O W
I C E   O A T   E X I L E
T R A C K   H U M P   M O R T
C U T E   M E R I T   P O O R
H E E L   E L I A   L Y N D A
      T R E S S   M A A   Y E P
      B U S   V I N C E
P A T   P Y L E   S K A T E R
S L E E P   A N E W   S U R E
S T A L L   C O L E   E N I D
T O M M Y   E M I R   L E N D
```

89

```
2074   3837   3101
3672  98449   3046
4273  43983   4003
69170   0824959
    7225687
849  0017  22287
7554  2440  31389
3950298  0032347
21240  5137  0477
 05275  1012  456
    4031799
7278143  34125
3365  84235  8322
0695  43647  1254
4852   4010  0259
```

90

```
OTHER  MINT  PONE
PROBE  ALAS  AVID
RUMBA  DIRK  GENE
ACE  GEER  KORAN
HERBAL   ACID
   OHO  STOWAWAY
MADRAS  TONI  HUE
OLEG  SCARF  SODA
SEA  LAHR  REPAIR
TENDERER   OWE
   RAYE  NEWMAN
STROP  RAFT  EVA
MEOW  PILL  SEDAN
OLDS  INGE  AGAIN
GLEE  EGAD  DOLLY
```

91

```
LOOK  TIER  WATT
IDLE  ARDOR  ACRE
SIGN  TEASE  RHEA
PEANUT  MID  SEEK
   ENOS  EDNA
 HADDOCK  IOWAN
TOKYO  ROAST  DIP
ORR  PORCH  ALE
ONO  ELDER  ADMEN
 ENEMY  AIMLESS
   FOWL  DUDE
CLEF  OAF  TOPPER
HERO  OMAHA  EAVE
ODOR  DAMON  SCAN
PAST  SENT  TENT
```

92

```
SLOPS  EDIT  CADE
HOVEL  SORE  OREL
ORATE  SEAM  CALS
DEL  EWER  PHOBIA
   APEX  CEE
MERYL  TIRE  BAT
TAXI  STAR  PAULA
OPUS  HITCH  DRIP
ALDER  BEAU  URGE
DEE  EVER  NYLON
   LET  SCAT
MELVYN  JOHN  TOW
ALOE  IVAN  KEITH
SLUR  CAIN  ERNIE
SADA  ELLY  ERASE
```

93

R	A	I	L		M	A	A		S	C	A	N	T	Y
O	B	O	E		A	D	D		C	A	M	E	R	A
S	U	N	G		E	R	A		A	N	I	M	A	L
S	T	E	I	N		I	M	P	L	Y		O	P	E
			T	I	F	F		U	P	O	N			
A	S	P		C	U	T	E	R		N	A	I	V	E
L	A	R	D	E	R		A	S	K		S	N	O	B
E	R	I	E		O	F	T	E	N		A	L	T	O
R	A	Z	E		R	U	E		E	I	L	E	E	N
T	H	E	D	A		D	R	Y	E	R		T	R	Y
			S	W	I	G		E	L	A	M			
E	S	S		A	R	E	N	A		N	A	N	C	Y
R	E	M	A	K	E		E	R	E		Y	O	R	E
L	A	U	R	E	N		E	L	K		O	R	A	L
E	N	G	I	N	E		D	Y	E		R	A	M	P

94

F	E	E	L		O	A	T	E	R		D	E	S	I
L	A	N	E		P	R	I	M	E		A	N	K	A
A	S	T	A		T	O	N	I	C		R	A	I	N
S	T	I	R		S	E	R	I	A	L				
H	E	R		W	E	E			P	L	A	S	M	A
	R	E	M	I	T		S	E	E	D		T	I	N
			A	L	C	O	T	T		A	G	E	N	T
A	L	M	S		H	U	R	O	N		O	P	I	E
R	I	A	T	A		S	A	N	I	T	Y			
E	L	L		C	I	T	Y		C	E	A	S	E	
S	O	L	E	M	N		U	K	E		A	D	A	
			L	E	S	S	E	N		S	L	I	D	
S	H	A	M		E	L	A	T	E		L	U	T	E
H	O	L	E		R	E	S	I	N		A	T	O	P
H	E	I	R		T	W	E	E	D		P	E	R	T

95

D	R	A	M		M	A	Y	S		V	I	S	T	A
R	E	B	A		A	R	E	A		A	S	K	E	R
I	R	O	N		S	E	A	L		T	R	I	A	L
N	U	D	N	I	K		R	A	P		A	M	M	O
K	N	E	A	D		I	N	M	A	T	E			
				E	A	T		I	S	O	L	A	T	E
O	R	B		A	R	C	H		S	P	I	N	E	T
M	I	L			S	H	O	O	K			T	E	N
A	P	A	C	H	E		G	W	E	N		I	N	A
R	E	B	O	U	N	D		E	Y	E				
			S	H	A	R	O	N		A	S	P	E	N
S	L	A	T		L	A	P		A	T	T	I	L	A
T	A	T	U	M		W	E	A	N		R	A	F	T
A	R	O	M	A		E	R	I	N		U	N	I	T
T	A	M	E	R		R	A	R	E		T	O	N	Y

96

K	N	A	V	E		E	N	O	S		B	L	E	W
E	A	S	E	L		P	I	N	E		R	A	V	I
E	T	H	E	L		I	G	O	R		I	D	E	S
N	E	E		I	N	C	H		P	A	D	D	L	E
			R	O	E			B	E	R	G			
E	N	T	I	T	L	E		E	N	M	E	S	H	
G	A	R	B		L	I	G	H	T		S	T	Y	E
A	V	A			T	O	E			R	E	B		
D	A	D	A		W	H	O	L	E		L	E	N	A
	L	E	S	L	I	E		D	U	N	A	W	A	Y
			P	U	R	R		R	U	B				
O	B	L	I	G	E		L	O	O	T		T	A	N
T	O	U	R		T	H	E	N		M	A	R	I	O
T	O	R	I		A	U	N	T		E	B	E	R	T
O	M	E	N		P	E	S	O		G	E	E	S	E

97

H	O	U	N	D		S	T	O	P		S	P	E	W
A	R	T	I	E		T	R	U	E		P	O	L	E
S	C	A	P	E		A	I	R	Y		I	L	K	A
H	A	H		P	U	N	K		T	E	L	L	E	R
			S	E	N	S	E		O	W	L			
	A	P	A	R	T			O	N	E		A	L	F
P	O	E	M		O	L	E	G		R	E	G	A	L
A	R	A	B		O	A	R		R	I	T	E		
A	T	L	A	S		O	R	E	L		A	L	E	E
R	A	E		I	N	K		E	S	S	E	X		
			P	L	Y		S	P	A	C	E			
C	O	S	E	L	L		N	I	N	A		T	A	D
O	V	E	R		O	P	A	L		R	O	U	S	E
T	A	L	K		N	E	R	O		E	R	N	I	E
E	L	L	Y		S	A	L	T		D	R	E	A	M

98

P	A	I	D		C	A	S	S		A	L	O	H	A
E	L	S	E		A	M	E	N		L	A	P	E	L
K	A	L	E		N	I	L	E		U	S	U	A	L
E	N	E	R	G	Y		F	R	O	M		S	T	Y
			E	R	O	S		D	I	N				
S	P	A		A	N	E	W		N	I	C	H	E	
P	E	S	C	I		W	E	A	K		H	E	A	P
O	R	I	O	N		E	B	B		J	E	R	R	Y
T	I	D	E		W	R	E	N		A	T	O	L	L
	L	E	D	G	E		R	E	A	M		D	Y	E
			A	L	E		R	E	I	N				
E	E	L		S	L	A	B		R	E	A	L	T	Y
C	R	E	A	K		T	O	N	I		I	O	W	A
H	I	N	G	E		E	L	I	A		V	A	I	L
O	C	T	E	T		R	O	L	L		E	D	G	E

99

E	A	R	L		P	E	S	T	O		C	A	S	K
P	L	E	A		A	C	T	O	R		O	B	O	E
S	L	A	W		P	R	A	N	K		G	L	U	T
O	I	L		G	A	U	G	E		K	N	E	L	T
M	E	M	O	R	Y		R	H	E	A				
			L	E	A	P	T		U	R	C	H	I	N
F	L	A	G	G		O	A	T	E	R		E	R	A
L	A	V	A		M	U	S	H	Y		F	R	A	N
U	N	O		T	O	R	T	E		L	E	O	N	A
E	D	W	A	R	D		E	M	B	E	R			
			D	I	E	T		I	N	N	I	N	G
C	H	A	R	M		A	D	A	N	O		V	I	A
H	A	L	O		B	L	O	N	D		W	A	N	T
A	U	D	I		R	O	U	T	E		I	N	T	O
P	L	O	T		A	N	G	E	R		L	A	H	R

100

8	7	4	1		8	9	2	2		1	8	4	1
6	6	3	2		9	9	9	9	0		1	0	8	5
4	1	5	2		3	3	2	2	2		9	1	4	4
9	1	9	6	9	8		0	2	8	3	4	3	7
			3	9	4	3	9	5	6				
3	9	1		0	8	3	3		2	1	3	2	6
4	7	5	8		6	7	1		0	9	5	8	3	2
7	0	6	9	9		4	7	8		0	6	4	4	1
3	0	8	8	7	9		2	7	1		2	7	5	7
	5	2	2	2	8		3	6	7	8		7	2	8
			3	4	7	0	9	7	1				
6	9	1	2	3	6	4		0	7	2	0	5	0
6	6	3	7		3	4	4	3	1		2	5	2	8
8	9	5	0		8	5	7	3	6		3	9	9	7
1	0	9	6		9	7	9	3		6	4	3	4

310

101

B	O	R	N		B	L	A	H			M	A	L	L
A	R	E	A		R	Y	D	E	R		I	D	E	A
B	A	N	G		E	N	O	L	A		R	A	V	I
A	T	E		I	N	N		P	Y	R	A	M	I	D
R	E	W	A	R	D			M	A	G				
		G	O	A	L		H	O	N	E	S	T	Y	
C	R	O	O	N		E	V	E	N	T		P	I	E
R	A	N	G		G	R	I	N	D		V	I	L	A
O	U	T		N	A	O	M	I		M	E	T	E	R
	C	L	O	S	E	L	Y		E	D	I	T		
				P	A	L		I	N	S	T	E	P	
C	A	B	A	R	E	T		S	O	X		R	E	O
A	F	A	R		O	R	S	O	N		S	A	R	I
I	R	I	S		N	O	L	A	N		O	D	I	N
N	O	T	E			T	Y	P	E		B	E	E	T

102

B	A	E	Z		F	E	A	R			M	A	I	L
E	R	L	E		C	L	A	R	E		E	L	S	A
A	L	M	A		O	A	T	E	S		L	I	A	R
T	O	O	L	B	O	X		S	E	E		G	A	R
		O	A	K			A	G	E	N	C	Y		
N	O	S	T	R	I	L		S	L	A	V			
O	P	T		E	N	A	C	T		D	E	B	U	T
V	E	A	L		G	U	A	R	D		N	A	P	A
A	N	N	O	Y		G	L	O	R	Y		L	O	N
			P	O	S	H		P	E	E	P	I	N	G
		T	O	P	E	K	A		S	A	Y			
E	L	L		O	N	O		A	S	H	T	R	A	Y
A	L	E	C		E	A	G	L	E		H	U	L	A
C	I	A	O		S	T	E	E	R		O	D	O	R
H	E	D	Y			T	H	E	E		N	E	E	D

103

J	U	M	B	O			S	T	E	M		G	A	D
A	R	O	U	N	D		E	A	V	E		R	U	E
D	A	N	G	E	R		A	B	E	D		E	R	R
A	L	A	S		O	S	L	O		I	O	W	A	N
			I	N	K		O	M	A	R				
I	T	S		R	E	E	K		U	N	D	E	R	
T	I	A	R	A		W	E	S	T		E	L	A	M
E	D	N	A		R	E	B	U	T		A	I	D	E
M	A	T	T		A	R	A	B		A	L	T	A	R
	L	A	T	I	N		B	L	A	B		E	R	E
			A	N	K	A		E	W	E				
B	L	A	N	C		P	I	T	A		D	O	L	T
E	E	K		O	R	A	L		R	A	I	D	E	R
T	A	I		M	O	R	K		D	I	V	I	N	E
A	N	N		E	T	T	A			R	E	E	S	E

104

A	G	L	O	W		E	L	I	A		P	H	I	L
B	L	A	D	E		V	E	R	B		R	A	R	E
B	A	B	E	L		E	W	E	R		O	V	E	N
O	R	E		D	A	L	I		O	S	M	O	N	D
T	E	L	L	E	R		S	L	A	W		C	E	L
			E	R	I	N		I	D	O	L			
S	C	A	D		D	E	M	O		R	A	B	I	D
T	O	N	G	S		W	O	N		E	R	O	D	E
Y	O	D	E	L		A	M	E	N		E	B	A	Y
			R	O	A	R		L	O	A	D			
A	D	D		P	I	K	E		S	N	O	R	E	D
D	R	I	V	E	R		L	E	E	K		E	L	I
M	O	V	E		M	A	L	T		L	A	G	E	R
I	V	A	N		E	D	E	N		E	D	I	C	T
T	E	N	D		N	A	N	A		T	E	S	T	Y

105

```
E L A T E   G A S H   H A T
R O B I N   P I N T O   A L I
I D E A L   E L T O N   B A G
E E L   A S S A I L   M I M E
      E C H O   E D I T O R
L A W Y E R   A B N E R
A C H E   E L L E   L A M A S
U M A   W A L E S   A S P
D E T E R   D E F T   B Y T E
      M O L D Y   A F R A I D
M A R I N A   A R I A
E X I T   Y O G U R T   W E T
A I L   E M B E D   F I E R Y
R O E   L E O N I   U N P I N
A M Y   K N E E   L A T K E
```

106

```
A N T E   A T O M   P A S S
A I R S   N I L E S   O P A L
H A Y S   Y E A S T   L O W E
      E M O   F A R M   L Y E
F L A X E N   E A G L E T
L I L   T E L L   E R R O R
A F I R E   E L A P S E
P E T E   D O W   E V E R
      P A P A Y A   A T A R I
D E L H I   D Y A N   S I C
C A N Y O N   S N I T C H
O L D   Y A L E   H E N
B L I P   T O R S O   L U M P
R A V E   A R M O R   A S I A
A S E A   D A N E   Y E L L
```

107

```
O B E Y   M O S S   S C R A P
C O M O   A L T O   P A U L A
T O O K   R E A L   A S S E T
E N T O M B   G O O   I T C H
T E E   E L K E   N A N
      O W E N   S N O O T Y
S O F A   I N L E T   L O U
H A L F   A F O O T   C E L L
O H O   E V E R T   O G L E
P U E B L O   T H A N
      A M I   S O O N   A R C
P L A Y   D O N   S Y M B O L
L O G I C   M I T T   E A S E
O R O N O   E D I E   S T I R
P I G G Y   N E L L   S E E K
```

108

```
A L T A R   F I S H   E C R U
F O R T Y   L O C O   G L E N
A G A T E   A T O P   G I G I
R O P E   G A T E S   M A T
      S U N G   T A B L E
C A S T R O   R A O U L
A L L   N O T A R Y   U R A L
R E E L   D A N E S   M A K O
R E D O   L O C A T E   V I N
      F L E S H   E R R I N G
C A C T I   C R E E
E R A   D O B I E   T A T E
L E N A   M O L D   J U L I A
E N O S   A N K A   O R D E R
B A N K   R E A R   G N A R L
```

109

H	E	A	R	T		C	R	A	B		V	A	M	P
O	L	D	I	E		H	A	I	L		E	V	E	L
E	L	O	P	E		E	Y	R	E		T	A	R	A
			T	R	E	E		A	S	S	I	G	N	
A	H	A		H	E	P		A	C	T		L	E	E
C	O	B	W	E	B		A	S	H	E	N			
I	G	O	R		A	L	A	N		A	I	D	E	
D	A	V	I	S		A	R	E		L	E	I	G	H
	N	E	S	T		B	O	R	G		C	A	R	E
			T	A	L	O	N		W	I	E	N	E	R
R	O	D		C	U	R		P	E	R		A	T	E
O	Z	A	R	K	S		D	I	N	O				
B	O	N	O		T	O	I	L		N	O	B	E	L
O	N	T	O		E	D	N	A		I	N	A	N	E
T	E	E	M		R	E	E	F		C	O	N	D	O

110

8	0	6	9		2	6	4	3	1		5	3	4	7
8	6	8	7		0	3	9	7	4		0	2	9	8
1	3	4	4		3	0	1	3	2		0	8	3	3
5	8	1	0	0		8	3	3	0	7		5	3	5
			7	4	1	3		4	8	0	4	5	2	
8	6	2	9	4	6		1	5	2	3	2			
1	5	7		1	0	4	8	5		5	3	9	1	1
0	9	0			0	0	0			8	6	0		
2	8	1	4	0		0	8	3	2	5		0	7	1
			1	4	4	1	8		2	6	4	7	2	0
9	1	7	9	1	1		3	1	2	3				
6	8	1		6	8	5	5	2		2	4	9	2	6
4	8	2	7		4	2	6	5	4		9	0	6	9
3	9	6	2		3	7	8	4	0		8	5	9	6
8	8	5	9		5	2	6	2	5		2	9	9	8

111

D	R	I	L	L		R	A	S	P		R	O	S	A
R	E	N	E	E		A	U	T	O		E	D	A	M
A	N	G	S	T		D	R	E	W		V	I	N	E
T	O	A	S	T		I	A	N		L	I	N	E	N
			E	G	O		O	P	I	E				
C	A	I	R	O				O	N	W	A	R	D	
B	A	R	R		B	E	H	O	L	D		B	E	E
O	P	R	A	H		R	O	O		A	G	I	L	E
L	E	A		E	A	R	T	H	Y		A	D	A	M
T	R	Y	I	N	G				E	S	S	E	X	
			O	R	E	L		A	P	T				
S	T	U	D	Y		O	I	L		I	D	L	E	R
T	O	N	I		A	U	N	T		T	I	A	R	A
E	R	I	N		N	I	C	E		C	R	O	O	K
P	E	T	E		D	E	A	R		H	E	S	S	E

112

D	U	E	T		A	G	R	E	E		O	L	G	A
O	G	L	E		R	E	E	S	E		M	E	A	L
E	L	S	E		K	N	A	C	K		I	N	F	O
R	Y	A	N		U	M	A		S	T	I	F	F	
			Y	O	G	I		P	A	N		N	E	T
A	S	P		P	U	N		E	N	I	D			
S	H	U	T	E	Y	E		E	N	T	I	T	L	E
I	O	N	E								S	O	O	T
A	P	T	N	E	S	S		U	N	I	C	O	R	N
			T	A	K	E		P	E	N		T	I	A
B	R	R		S	I	C		S	E	A	R			
L	O	O	S	E		T	I	C		O	A	T	H	
I	S	L	E		A	I	D	A	N		O	B	E	Y
M	I	L	L		M	O	O	L	A		S	L	A	M
P	E	E	L		I	N	L	E	T		T	E	R	N

113

O	B	A	M	A		P	E	R	M		B	A	S	H
V	A	L	O	R		A	S	E	A		E	C	H	O
E	L	D	E	R		S	P	A	R		A	R	I	A
N	I	A		E	A	S	Y		A	W	N	I	N	G
			A	S	H	E		I	C	E		D	E	Y
I	N	C	I	T	E		G	N	A	S	H			
L	A	H	R		A	G	O	G		T	A	S	T	E
S	I	A	M		D	R	O	O	L		R	O	A	R
A	L	T	A	R		A	S	T	A		D	O	L	L
			N	U	R	S	E		T	H	E	N	C	E
E	S	S		L	A	P		S	H	I	N			
R	A	C	K	E	T		S	H	E	A		E	L	F
I	R	O	N		I	D	E	A		T	A	L	I	A
C	A	N	E		N	O	E	L		U	N	I	F	Y
A	N	E	W		G	E	N	T		S	T	A	T	E

114

J	O	B		C	L	A	M	P		S	O	M	E
A	R	E		K	R	A	M	E	R		T	R	O	D
N	O	G		L	I	V	E	L	Y		I	C	O	N
E	N	A		I	N	A	N	E		L	A	N	A
T	O	N	I	N	G		D	E	B	U	T		
		N	E	E	D		U	P	S	H	O	T
P	E	S	T		R	H	I	N	O		A	X	E
I	D	I	O	M		O	U	R		N	I	V	E	N
E	G	G		A	L	P	H	A		L	E	N	D
D	Y	N	A	M	O		N	O	O	K		
		C	A	N	O	E		L	I	A	B	L	E
A	L	E	C		S	N	A	I	L		L	I	L
H	O	A	R		A	C	T	I	V	E		A	T	E
E	C	R	U		L	A	R	D	E	R		D	E	N
M	O	P	E		F	R	Y	E	R		E	R	A

115

C	E	S	A	R		H	A	I	R		H	E	R	O
E	V	A	D	E		E	L	K	E		I	V	A	N
D	E	C	A	F		E	D	E	N		N	A	M	E
E	L	K		U	N	D	O		O	D	D			
			S	T	U		W	O	U	L	D			
T	O	W	E	L		S	A	N	D		A	I	L	
P	A	P	A		L	E	E	R		D	A	R	L	A
O	M	E	N		R	O	E		D	E	L	I		
L	A	N	K	Y		M	U	S	H		O	D	O	R
O	L	E		O	R	A	L		A	A	R	O	N	
			E	R	O	D	E		U	S	E			
		R	A	P		A	L	L	Y		T	A	D	
W	A	R	D		E	D	I	E		L	O	R	N	E
E	R	I	E		A	U	D	I		U	N	I	T	E
D	I	O	R		L	E	A	F		M	O	P	E	D

116

H	I	N	D	I		E	G	A	D		S	C	A	T
A	L	I	E	N		J	I	V	E		M	A	Y	A
L	I	N	E	N		E	L	A	M		I	T	E	M
T	E	E		I	N	C	A		O	P	T			
			K	N	I	T		S	T	E	E	L	E	
F	L	A	G	G		W	E	E		A	N	D		
B	R	E	T		H	I	D	E		N	O	R	M	A
L	O	N	I		M	U	D		P	I	E	R		
A	L	G	E	R		A	B	E	L		E	A	S	T
H	I	T		H	A	G		E	A	R	T	H		
		C	H	E	E	S	E		R	I	T	A		
			E	A	T		M	E	A	T		F	A	R
E	M	I	R		R	U	I	N		A	B	A	T	E
L	I	L	I		A	N	N	E		C	A	R	O	N
L	A	K	E		Y	O	K	E		H	A	R	P	O

117

D	U	M	P		D	I	A	L		A	S	K	E	W
A	R	E	A		I	N	G	E		M	I	R	T	H
D	A	R	N		G	A	I	N		P	R	I	C	E
S	L	E	E	V	E		L	A	N	E		S	H	E
			I	S	L	E			O	R	E			
	S	H	A	N	T	Y		L	E	S	S	O	N	
C	H	O	P		N	A	N	A		C	A	V	E	
R	A	M	P		A	D	M	A	N		A	L	E	X
A	L	E	E		D	A	I	S		P	O	R	T	
G	E	R	A	L	D		A	S	C	E	N	T		
			R	U	E		A	L	M	A				
S	I	S		G	R	A	B		O	N	W	A	R	D
A	D	A	N	O		M	I	L	O		A	L	O	E
D	O	R	I	S		E	D	I	T		C	A	L	F
A	L	I	B	I		S	E	T	H		O	N	L	Y

118

M	I	N	I		A	M	I	D		M	A	D	A	M
O	V	A	L		N	O	N	E		U	S	A	G	E
P	A	S	S		K	E	E	N		S	P	U	R	T
E	N	T	A	I	L		P	Y	L	E		N	E	E
R	A	Y		N	E	W	T		O	U	S	T	E	R
			A	S	T	A		M	A	M	E			
A	B	A	S	E		L	O	O	M		P	E	E	L
F	I	R	S	T		L	I	Z		S	T	A	L	E
T	O	F	U		S	E	L	A		A	E	R	I	E
			M	A	T	T		R	O	U	T			
S	L	E	E	T	Y		S	T	U	N		A	R	T
M	A	R		T	E	S	H		T	A	I	L	O	R
A	G	A	T	E		C	A	L	L		R	I	P	E
R	E	S	I	N		O	P	I	E		O	V	E	N
T	R	E	A	D		W	E	P	T		N	E	R	D

119

O	R	E	L		H	O	P	S		S	P	I	T	
R	E	N	E		A	O	R	T	A		T	I	T	O
A	L	D	A		W	H	E	E	L		E	A	S	Y
T	E	E	N	Y		S	T	A	T	E				
E	N	A		E	A	T	S		M	O	R	T	A	R
	T	R	E	A	T	Y		D	O	G		A	L	E
			S	H	O	R	T	Y		A	C	R	I	D
S	T	O	P		M	A	I	N	E		O	T	T	O
T	A	N	Y	A		N	E	A	T	E	R			
A	P	T		H	U	T		M	O	N	A	C	O	
R	E	O	P	E	N		B	O	N	O		H	I	S
			E	M	C	E	E		S	C	A	L	P	
B	O	A	R		L	A	R	G	E		O	N	C	E
E	R	I	K		E	R	R	O	R		S	C	A	N
A	R	M	Y		N	A	T	E		T	E	N	D	

120

S	A	S	H	A		M	A	P		A	T	L	A	S
K	N	E	A	D		A	D	A		R	O	A	S	T
I	N	A	N	E		N	A	N		C	O	N	T	E
T	A	N	G		S	N	I	T	C	H		D	I	M
			A	L	T	A	R		A	I	R			
M	A	R	I	E		P	R	E	A	C	H			
S	O	D		A	P	P	A	L	L		F	R	A	N
I	D	L	E	R		O	L	E		S	T	E	V	E
P	E	A	T		U	N	L	A	C	E		D	E	W
			L	I	T	A	N	Y		A	A	R	O	N
			A	R	I		T	A	S	T	E			
P	E	W		A	T	T	E	S	T		C	A	S	S
S	C	R	U	B		I	N	K		M	I	N	E	O
S	H	A	R	I		R	O	E		A	P	T	E	R
T	O	P	I	C		E	R	R		D	E	E	R	E

121

1 0 9 3		6 0 1		5 5 1 6
0 7 9 2	5 8 2 4 7	7 9 8 1
5 1 4 9	3 5 5 2 5	2 4 1 7
0 2 0 3 2 2	5 8 6 4 2	
8 7 3	5 1 8	9 3 4 5 5 9
9 7 9 0 1 2	2 8 0	6 9 2
4 3 5 0 2 8	7 5 8 4 6
1 9 8 9	3 9 5	5 2 2 1
6 2 6 6 0	8 9 8 0 6 7
1 7 4	3 9 8	1 0 4 9 3 5
7 1 9 3 8 3	1 9 1	6 4 5
3 6 4 6 4	0 9 8 0 1 6
9 8 5 2	8 0 8 3 1	8 2 6 6
9 3 8 1	6 2 3 0 7	8 2 1 0
6 8 3 7	7 3 7	2 0 9 0

122

I T E M	M A K O		P E N C E
D A N A	A D A M	I V O R Y
E B A Y	N O R A	S A V O R
A L C O T T	E R S T	A W E
L E T	E R I N	T O P
	E X A M	O L I V E R
S H O R T	P H E W	N I L E
L A W N	E L A T E	A S I A
A L E E	M Y T H	S T E A D
B O N S A I	I O T A
T I L	E C R U	H A S
A G O	R Y A N	A D J U S T
S U S H I	G O W N	E M I R
E L L E N	O L E G	S O D A
A L O N G	G A T E	T R E Y

123

P U M A		J I F F		S T U
I G O R	B E D L A M	Y E N
C H E R	E N L A C E	R A D
I R E	E G A D	U S E
C A V E	D I A P E R
L A M E N T	C L E A N
E B B	T I T H E	E D G Y
A L E C	P R O V E	W E R E
P E R U	A S I A N	L E A
R H Y M E	T E T H E R
P H O B I A	M A I D
R E D	T R E K	S O N
A N D	C R U I S E	K I L O
N I L	H O R N E T	E N I D
K E Y	W O K E	R A Z E

124

R A M B O	F I S T	B A T H
A L I E N	A R T E	E R I E
V A L V E	T A R P	L E E R
E N D	S Q U E A L
N I E C E	C E L	C O B
S W I G	A S K	S A L V E
N O T C H	K O R E A N
S A L E	A T A R I	C O L D
P R E M E D	R U M B A
A I D A N	D E N	O D I E
M A A	V E E	D E M U R
S Y M B O L	P R O
E P I C	B A B E	S C O O T
S A D A	E T O N	H A R P O
S T A R	D E E D	E N T E R

125

J	O	S	E		I	M	P		S	L	A	T
O	P	E	N		B	L	O	O	D		T	O	N	E
H	I	L	T		O	I	L	E	R		I	O	N	E
N	E	A	R		T	E	D		A	I	R	M	E	N
			A	H	A		Y	O	W	L
C	A	P	O	N	E		R	E	L	A	C	E
P	E	R		O	Y	S	T	E	R		D	R	A	G
A	L	O	F	T		K	E	G		G	A	U	G	E
D	E	M	I		W	I	N	O	N	A		E	L	M
B	A	N	T	A	M		N	O	Z	Z	L	E
			A	T	O	M		T	E	E
S	T	I	L	T	S		E	L	I		A	R	E	S
C	A	D	E		O	P	T	I	C		L	O	R	I
A	M	E	N		N	E	R	V	E		O	M	I	T
M	E	A	T		W	O	E		T	Y	K	E

125:
JOSE, IMP, SLAT
OPEN, BLOOD, TONE
HILT, OILER, IONE
NEAR, TED, AIRMEN
AHA, YOWL
CAPONE, RELACE
PER, OYSTER, DRAG
ALOFT, KEG, GAUGE
DEMI, WINONA, ELM
BANTAM, NOZZLE
ATOM, TEE
STILTS, ELI, ARES
CADE, OPTIC, LORI
AMEN, NERVE, OMIT
MEAT, WOE, TYKE

126:
KNOT, SPAR, APT
HAVE, COLLIE, PEA
APEX, OCELOT, ORR
NANA, MIA, HEROD
NOMAD, BEATTY
GYM, AIL, MARS
NOUGHT, HUH, TALL
ADIEU, DAD, DECOY
WARY, PAW, HORROR
SNUB, CEE, EKE
STREEP, DIARY
THERE, ERR, IFFY
REA, DETECT, ELLA
AID, YEARLY, LEAN
PRY, KNEE, DANK

127:

MEW, ESTEE, GLIB
AMI, UMPIRE, AURA
REP, NORMAL, NAIL
INEPT, YES, DUSK
ADROIT, REACH
REO, LOITER
ERIC, TILLER, ORE
LATHE, TEA, ASTIN
SIC, ASSIST, TEND
ADHERE, UTE
CLARA, XANADU
MALL, ELF, NOLAN
ELIA, INLAND, TIC
TONI, LEEWAY, ELL
SEER, KENNY, RYE

128:
LINER, THAI, MOD
ANIMAL, EARN, AXE
IGNITE, RICH, KEN
REAR, EMIT, AGONY
ICE, ISLE
CAD, THAN, AERATE
ADAPT, DOFF, ALAN
SOME, MOVIE, LILT
TROT, OWEN, ADAIR
SENIOR, LEST, SAY
TUNE, RUE
SWEET, STYE, ELMO
TOW, LOSE, DEVOUR
AVA, EDEN, ELAPSE
YEN, TEXT, KNEEL

129

```
EVA  ODD  TRESS
CLEM HER  HENNER
HARP OLE  ELAINE
EMBED HANOI DOE
     RESIDE SNERD
SATEEN    ASHE
PRO ROTATE  SOLE
UTAH OWNER SLUR
REDO ZINNIA ESS
   BEET  ALIGHT
SPOON  CHALET
TAP COHAN CACHE
EYELID RIP LEAR
MERINO STU IDLE
RAZOR HAG CEL
```

130

```
MAINE LOLA BEAR
EGRET ABED ACME
TEETH RIND RHEA
   NIVEN FROND
ASP IDA YULE
STANCE   MULCH
TARA ACCEPT RAM
ORATE RAW ELENA
RED DAYBED EDDY
 REIGN  ATTILA
RAYE TWO TEN
ARDOR DAUNT
BEAN FILM TABOO
BALI ITEM EBONY
EPIC THEY REPEL
```

131

```
INCA  URN  BELA
LEAD ARIES URAL
ILSA DINAH RAMP
ASIMOV GLEAN
DON DID BISTRO
 NOTICE BAR HEN
WEEVIL SKEET
DEMI ONO INFO
ADAGE TANGLE
DAY TIE DROVER
AMAZON EON SOP
 ENGEL VICTOR
SNOB OZONE LAKE
PAAR TRAIL OTIS
ANKA AMP DEES
```

132

```
0847  7256   7225
2451  05326  3902
9681  00667  2125
925179  3009  349
261  3342  275044
   4117  8556
21374  3717  0703
40208  659  57355
1493  0013  87722
   2130  0289
800430  2644  709
986  7613  243110
6077  18547  6807
4150  82828  7789
3118  2632  1769
```

133

K	A	R	L		C	L	U	B		C	A	S	E
E	R	I	E		A	L	A	M	O		H	O	W	L
A	L	V	A		R	E	R	A	N		A	R	E	A
N	E	E		A	G	O	G		S	E	P	T	E	T
U	N	T	I	D	Y		E	B	A	Y		A	P	E
			R	E	L	Y		A	I	D	A			
S	L	A	V		E	A	R	N		I	R	A	N	I
A	E	R	I	E		R	U	T		E	T	H	I	C
G	O	I	N	G		R	E	A	M		F	A	T	E
			G	Y	R	O		M	E	N	U			
L	A	S		P	A	W	N		T	O	L	E	D	O
A	L	C	O	T	T		E	W	E	R		L	E	S
D	O	O	M		I	D	A	H	O		I	D	E	S
L	U	R	E		O	U	T	E	R		T	E	R	I
E	D	E	N		N	E	O	N		T	R	E	E	

134

B	A	S	H		C	A	S	S		M	A	R	I	A
A	C	H	E		L	U	T	E		A	M	O	N	G
E	R	I	C		I	R	A	Q		L	I	T	E	R
R	E	N	T		M	A	N	U	A	L		O	P	E
			O	R	B		Z	E	E		A	R	T	E
S	H	A	R	E		W	A	L	R	U	S			
E	E	L		A	V	A		I	N	H	A	L	E	
A	R	M		D	E	Y		A	A	H		L	I	V
L	E	S	S	E	N		F	L	O		E	R	E	
			T	R	I	V	E	T		O	S	C	A	R
P	E	R	U		C	A	R		S	K	Y			
E	M	O		R	E	C	A	L	L		S	T	A	T
D	I	S	C	O		A	S	I	A		T	A	L	E
A	L	I	A	S		T	E	E	N		E	M	M	A
L	Y	N	D	A		E	R	S	T		M	E	A	L

135

J	O	A	N		G	A	S	P		S	C	O	F	F
A	M	M	O		R	I	L	E		E	A	T	E	R
V	A	I	N		O	D	O	R		E	S	T	E	E
A	R	D	E	N	T		S	I	T		T	O	D	D
			U	T	A	H		O	I	L				
E	G	G	N	O	G		E	N	D	E	A	R		
E	L	I	A		L	O	U	I	E		P	O	E	
B	I	L	G	E		E	A	R		A	B	A	S	E
B	O	D		A	B	A	T	E		E	R	I	K	
		T	A	L	C	U	M		K	A	R	A	T	E
			O	H	O		E	A	S	E				
S	C	A	T		Y	A	P		Y	O	N	D	E	R
L	U	C	I	D		B	O	I	L		A	R	L	O
A	R	M	O	R		E	C	R	U		P	A	L	M
W	E	E	N	Y		T	H	E	M		A	W	A	Y

136

I	D	L	E		E	D	D	I	E		L	I	S	T
L	O	A	N		N	O	R	M	A		A	S	T	I
K	E	P	T		A	D	A	P	T		T	R	O	T
			E	L	B	O	W		L	E	A	C	H	
C	O	R	R	A	L		L	O	S	E		E	K	E
A	W	E		C	E	E		R	E	A	L	L	Y	
L	E	D	G	E		X	A	N	A	D	U			
S	N	O	W		P	I	A		L	A	S	T		
			E	S	C	O	R	T		O	U	N	C	E
G	E	N	I	U	S		E	L	K		N	A	N	
S	A	M		F	R	E	T		O	R	I	E	N	T
C	R	E	S	T		A	S	I	A	N				
O	G	R	E		A	B	B	O	T		L	E	S	T
O	L	G	A		S	A	B	L	E		A	R	I	A
T	E	E	M		P	A	Y	E	R		Y	A	R	D

137

138

139